# transitions

Sandra Escontrias, with
Book Reviews by Lou Brakeman

## A Study for the Second Half of Life

# MISSION STATEMENT

*Autumn Saints is a Christ-centered organization whose mission is to provide written and web-based resources for second-half-of-life spirituality. These Bible-based materials are designed for use in safe and supportive small groups.*

*"Even when I am old and gray, do not forsake me, O God, till I declare your power to the next generation, your might to all who are to come."* PSALMS 71:18

# TRANSITIONS

Entering the new phase of our lives called Elderhood means meeting head-on the changes that are creeping (or in some cases barreling) into our lives as we age. We can only do this if we understand God's overall purpose for life on earth—fitting his beloved children for Kingdom life, both here on earth *and* in the hereafter. Understanding this helps us to recognize that we are not "going down hill" but are merely reaching a different stage in our growth that requires much of us and rewards us greatly.

We begin this life as dependent children. With a great deal of help we reach a maturity in which we assume care-taking responsibility for ourselves and others—our children and/or elderly parents. These years include meaningful work. During these years family networks are strengthened, broken down or redefined. Up to now, much of our self-worth has come from our work and accomplishments, what we possess, and what others think of us. Elderhood might bring a screeching halt to this vision of our worth. This stage of life may entail retirement from a long career of productive work, downsizing possessions and property, loss of a mate who may have provided our security and identity, and subjection to an ageism rampant in a society that overvalues youth and undervalues its elders. Failure to negotiate this transition may bring self-absorption and stagnation—often characterized by a critical nature, increasing levels of anger, and depression.

If we allow ourselves to accept a viewpoint that life is "indeed all downhill from 60 on" and wallow in self-pity for what we have lost, we are indeed miserable! BUT if we can see this as a shedding of our midlife skin so that new skin can hold our new growth, life becomes an adventure. We have important tasks to accomplish and wisdom to impart. The road ahead is not for sissies! Successfully negotiating this next step in our growth requires awareness, acceptance, and adjustments. A strong spiritual life (defined as a deep friendship with God) gives us courage, strength, hope, and a deep sense of meaning. In addition we have a responsibility to model this transition in such a way that it reduces fear and creates anticipation and HOPE in those who are coming along behind us!

Teenagers try hard to be identical to every other teen in their group by wearing the same clothes, listening to the same music, and holding the same opinions. Being different is considered a horrible cross to bear. But by the time we have reached our mature years we are comfortable being an "individual" and easily recognize that no other person has exactly the same experience or timetable.

God continues the work that he has begun in us. Often using the chiselling tools of downsizing, physical limitation, dependence, vulnerability and loss of control among others. If we deny or fight what is happening we miss the blessings of his work.

In this section of work, we also become aware that what God is doing is not only about us. Many of the things that happen to us become the shaping tools he uses on others—our children, our friends, our church, our community. Which of us would not rather be on the giving side of life? Receiving from others is very hard, yet how can we give if everyone is giving and there are no receivers? Our dependence can be a gift that we give over to others so that God may work in them using us. Scripture says that there is no greater love than to lay down our lives for our friends. Receiving others' giving to us with gracious appreciation is a gift that we give them with great love! It takes great spiritual maturity to find the balance between insisting on doing what we can continue to do and letting go and receiving the help we really need. If we are not careful, our pride can prod us to become angry at all we have lost. Receiving in love as Jesus received the gift of perfume from Mary, can be a great blessing to others and to ourselves if we will let it.

Come, join the journey of *Transitions*! It is indeed a challenging adventure.‡ [SCE]

# TRANSITIONS

*I will be glad and rejoice in your love, for you saw my affliction and knew the anguish of my soul. You have not handed me over to the enemy but have set my feet in a spacious place.*

*Psalm 31:7-8*

CHAPTER *1*

# HELP I'M GETTING OLD

**KEY THOUGHT: Recognizing and accepting that we are entering a new stage of life called Elderhood, will enable us to store up inner resources to draw on as the process of aging continues.**

Elderhood need not be threatening. Even though we confront many worrisome possibilities we know that God is with us in all that we encounter. There is nothing that can separate us from his love. We do, however, face many changes that come and we need to go through a process of transition and transformation if we are to reap all that God has for us. The world we live in would have us deny and cover up those things that remind us of our vulnerability. The ad men attempt to sell us things that will retain the appearance of youth. Really? They may make us feel or look younger, but do nothing to stop the march of years. We can do away with wrinkles and "spare tires" but the years will continue to mount no matter what we do to make it seem otherwise. Enevitably our eyes need glasses and our ears need help to hear. We will lose our friends and spouses. We will have to downsize and simplify our lives. While we can prolong the image of youth, we are still gathering years. Aging is a part of the natural process of the life which God has given to us. Therefore it is up to us to discover the riches that he has in store for us at this stage of life. An attitude of acceptance, a willingness to change and transform life as we now know it, a sense of adventure seeking what God has in store for us, will make these years ones of wonder and joy.

# LESSON 1, DAY 1
## THE FACE OF ELDERHOOD

**GRACE:** *To accept the realization that one is growing old.*

**SCRIPTURE:** Ecclesiastes 12:1-8

## MEDITATION QUESTIONS:

1) The writer gives us some vivid images of the physical effects of aging. Can you find them?

2) What are ways you can remember the Lord, the creator?

3) Do you think that these are typical things that happen to people as they age? Have some of them begun to happen to you?

## FOR YOUR CONSIDERATION:

Someone once told me that he planned to die before aging became an issue. Therefore he is doing nothing to preserve his body—no exercise, no blood pressure medicine, and no healthy eating for him. He is not so different from many who hope that they will die peacefully in their sleep having avoided all the challenges of elderhood. Most of us fight the process in every way we know. We see it happening to others and fervently pray that the difficulties of aging will give us a miss. And frankly who in their right mind hopes to be frail? We want long life but only if we have "quality of life" according to our own definitions. It is quite natural to dread the losses and fear the suffering that often come with aging. Scripture gives us examples of lament from people who feel the same way we do. Scripture does not ask us to deny our feelings and fears but to express them openly and aloud to our heavenly Father. Only after we have done this can we open ourselves to the resources available to receive all that he has for us in this time of life.

**FOR JOURNALING:** When I asked my Sunday School children how they could tell someone was old they were able to give me 17 indications. How many can you name? Which of these might you fear?

_____

_____

_____

_____

_____

_____

_____

_____

_____

_____

_____

_____

_____

_____

_____

_____

_____

_____

_____

_____

_____

_____

_____

_____

_____

_____

_____

_____

# LESSON 1, DAY 2
## GETTING IT OUT

**GRACE**: *That I might voice the aspects of aging that I dread or fear.*

**SCRIPTURE**: Psalm 88

## MEDITATION QUESTIONS:

1) What are some of the serious fears of aging that this psalm of lament addresses?

2) Most psalms that start with the negatives of life end with resounding faith in God. Why do you think this psalm has no such ending?

3) Which of these laments creates the most fear in you?

## FOR YOUR CONSIDERATION:

The author of this psalm addresses some very serious concerns of the aging—the loss of loved ones and friends, the nearness of death, the loss of strength and power, vulnerability, friends who no longer come around because they are repulsed by pain and suffering, the apparent absence of God, and coming judgment. Getting these fears out into the open releases us to find resources of strength, courage, love and even joy in the midst of these challenges. While there are some who seem to sail through their latter years, most of us will be called to depend on our inner resources in at least some of these areas. Now is the time to develop those resources. It is like putting money in the bank—better to do it before you need it. Many tell me they are not ready to confront aging. They are "not all that old." But if one waits to confront and build resources until they are needed, they may not have the physical or mental ability to do so. Just try to save money in the midst of an economic depression! Likewise just try to build inner resources in the midst of loss or pain. Now is the time to act.

**FOR JOURNALING:** What are the aspects of aging that you fear the most? What kind of inner resources might you need to cope with those things you fear?

_____

_____

_____

_____

_____

_____

_____

_____

_____

_____

_____

_____

_____

_____

_____

_____

_____

_____

_____

_____

_____

_____

_____

_____

_____

# LESSON 1, DAY 3
## BESEIGED

GRACE: *Continued grace to voice our fears about aging.*

SCRIPTURE: Psalm 31

## MEDITATION QUESTIONS:

1) What are the emotions that David is expressing?

2) In verse 9-13, David laments what his enemies are doing to him. What are his concerns? How might they apply to aging?

3) What are the resources that David is using to defeat his enemies? How might you use some of the same resources?

## FOR YOUR CONSIDERATION:

David is feeling beseiged. Everything is being mounted against him. We look at some of our elders and wonder how in the world they are coping. They are dealing with loss, loneliness, decreased income, physical inconvenience and disability all at the same time. They too seem beseiged. The view from outside does not coincide with what we see in their spirits. We often see peace, gentleness, courage, good humor, concern for others, and a deep love of God. How do they manage this? Like David their trust is in the Lord. This trust has been built over years of seeing God at work in their lives—becoming aware of his faithfulness, his compassion and love. Many already had a well to draw from in place. It did not happen over night. As things have happened to them, they have sought God's presence in their circumstances and have been drawn close to him as he gives comfort, strength and courage. During this process God lessens their hold on this earth and holds out the hope of the home he is preparing for them on the other side. "Be strong and take heart."

**FOR JOURNALING:** Describe an elderly person whom you know that appears to be beseiged, but whose inner resources shine through. Take time to ask them about those resources.

---
---
---
---
---
---
---
---
---
---
---
---
---
---
---
---
---
---
---
---
---
---
---
---
---
---
---

# LESSON 1, DAY 4
## LIGHT AND MOMENTARY TROUBLES

**GRACE:** *That others may see that our resources come from God not us.*

**SCRIPTURE:** 2 Corinthians 4:7-18

## MEDITATION QUESTIONS:

1) How does Paul explain the difficulties that are happening to him?

2) What are the things seen? What are the things unseen?

3) How might the faith of the aging person show forth God rather than themselves?

## FOR YOUR CONSIDERATION:

We have been very focused on the seen things of life—our physical needs and appearance, our work, our family, the things we do in service and for pleasure. We might believe in the unseen but seldom look for it. Who would normally look for beauty in a worn out pot? Yet Paul tells us that we have the wonderful renewing Spirit of the Lord in bodies that are wasting away. In fact we are being renewed inwardly day by day. It is like a plaster mold in which an artist is pouring beautiful bronze or gold. As the mold is being handled and filled, it begins to deteriorate on the outside. When the outer is finally torn away the inward beauty is exposed. In our society we keep trying to repair the mold and our excessive concern for the outside may hinder the Artist from filling the shabby mold with his beauty. As outside activities and responsibilities tend to slow down, God uses a refiner's fire to purify the gold within. He burns away the dross and centers our hearts and minds on what really matters.

**FOR JOURNALING:** Which gets more of your attention, the outer or the inner—the seen or the unseen? If your physical parts were pulled away, would there still be life in your inner parts? Why or why not?

_____

_____

_____

_____

_____

_____

_____

_____

_____

_____

_____

_____

_____

_____

_____

_____

_____

_____

_____

_____

_____

_____

# LESSON 1, DAY 5
## HOPE IN THE LORD

**GRACE:** *To be filled with hope in the Lord.*

**SCRIPTURE:** Psalm 146

**MEDITATION QUESTIONS:**

1) What does the psalmist tell us are the wrong places in which to place our trust?

2) What does the Lord do for his people?

3) Which of these activities of the Lord can bring hope for those in elderhood?

**FOR YOUR CONSIDERATION:**

Many people seem to place their hope in the "miracles" of modern medicine. They expect a cure for cancer, a treatment for alzheimer's, new replacement bones and joints, a discovery which will allow organs to regenerate. If only they can hold on to what they have for as long as they can science will find the answer to the problems of aging, extending both quality and quantity of life. Scripture tells us over and over that our hope is not in this world. Our hope is in the Lord, the maker of heaven and earth. God has a plan to give us a new earth and heaven, a new body like unto the risen body of Christ, but we rewrite the script and look for the answers in this life, in this body, and in the "princes" of this world. His inner work is preparing us for eternal life. This eternal life begins in the here and now and extends beyond our deaths. The psalmist tells us to hope in the Lord. It is he who will uphold the cause of the oppressed, feed the hungry, give sight to the blind, lift up those who are bowed down, watches over the alien and stranger, sustains the fatherless and the widow(er) for all generations. Only he can give us eternity.

**FOR JOURNALING:** As you look forward to advanced aging, where does your hope lie? Escape? Science? Religion? The mercy and compassion of God?

_____

_____

_____

_____

_____

_____

_____

_____

_____

_____

_____

_____

_____

_____

_____

_____

_____

_____

_____

_____

_____

_____

_____

_____

_____

# A MAN TALKING TO HIS HOUSE

### By JALAL AD-DIN RUMI

*I say that no one in this caravan is awake
and that while you sleep, a thief is stealing*

*the signs and symbols of what you thought
was your life. Now you're angry with me for*

*telling you this! Pay attention to those who
hurt your feelings telling you the truth.*

*Giving and absorbing compliments is like
trying to paint on water, that insubstantial.*

*Here is how a man once talked with his house,
"Please, if you're ever about to collapse,*

*let me know." One night without a word the
house fell. "What happened to our agreement?"*

*The house answered, "Day
and night I've been
telling you with cracks and
broken boards and*

*holes appearing like mouths
opening. But you
kept patching and filling those
with mud, so*

*proud of your stopgap mason-
ry. You didn't
listen." This house is your
body always*

*saying, I'm leaving; I'm going
soon. Don't
hide from one who knows the
secret.*

18

# A FINAL WORD—AGAINST THE FLOW

What makes growing old so difficult? Aging requires us to go against the flow of cultural norms and expectations—maybe even or especially our own expectations. Senior adults are much like the salmon that has to swim upstream. Here are just a few examples.

*Accumulation vs. downsizing*

Our whole society is based on accumulation and consumerism. Hourly we are bombarded with advertisements of products that we "simply must have" to make our lives complete. Products are quickly outdated so that new ones can take their place. We are encouraged to buy, buy, buy in order to help keep our economy strong. Merchants are like sirens, drawing us into their stores with special discounts, sales, and services. HOWEVER most senior adults need to downsize and "get rid of stuff." They no longer have the need, income, desire, or energy to purchase and maintain all that "stuff." It's amazing how out of it you can feel when you are unable to talk about your latest acquisition. And it is painful to let go of things that have memories and meaning. On the bright side, downsizing encourages good stewardship, communal sharing, and passing our material heritage on to others.

*Collagen vs. wrinkles, sags, and liver spots*

Look at any magazine and you will know that beauty is equated with youth. Even magazines geared toward senior adults use models that are superfit and appear young for their age. Article after article talks about how to put off, cover up, or surgically remove the signs of aging. While it used to be only the very wealthy or those glamorous aging superstars who underwent the knife, today anyone who is aging is encouraged to consider this option. Mature adults wise enough to accept that drastic efforts to appear young are only delaying the inevitable, will need to stand firm against the flood secure in the knowledge that while the body is showing signs of breaking down the inner spirit is alive and well, maturing in qualities of compassion and wisdom. This mature inner self graces the world with a beauty that reaches deeper than mere sexual titillation.

*Independence vs. interdependence and dependence*

Do you have your own TV in your own room with your own remote? Can you cool the air on your side of the car to your own personal body temperature? Then you are living the American life of individualism.

God forbid that we should have to compromise or share! Ours is a country of the "self-made" man (or woman). Americans do not want to depend on anyone else for anything. Asking for or requiring help is like dental surgery without the Novocain. Many would rather sit in the dark than have to ask someone to put in a new light bulb for them. Others would rather sit alone at home than ask for a ride to a special function. AND we certainly don't want our children to be burdened with us (or we with them). But aging forces us from independence to first becoming interdependent and then often dependent—if not on our own family then on those that we have paid to meet our needs. Dependency goes against the grain of everything we have worked for.

Christian community is largely based on interdependence/dependence. We are meant to give and take. Most of us have the giving down pat. But when it comes to receiving, we balk. One of the greatest gifts we can give is to receive gracefully the gifts that others have to offer us. In receiving the help of others we are giving them the gift of being needed, the gift of inner warmth in helping another, and encouragement to be even more giving at the next opportunity.

### Doing vs. being

Upon reaching maturity, our identity has largely been based on what we do. Attend any social function and the introductory question is "What do you do?" Many seniors fill their hours with activities so that they can still answer this question. "I'm busier now than when I worked." "I play bridge." "I serve at the food pantry." "I do." "I do." "I do." While we may have many years after retirement from paid work in which we can still do many things, as time passes we are able to do less. Aging requires us to become more interior and the transition for many is very difficult.

Our true identity comes, not from what we do, but from the knowledge that we are a beloved child of God. Through prayer and meditation it is possible to maintain a growing and rich relationship with God. Our identity is firmly established in His love.

Looking at just these few examples, it is easier to understand why "aging is not for sissies." It takes intentional effort to maintain a healthy perspective, understand and reap the benefits of aging, and experience positive relationships with others as we age. Going against the flow and accepting these changes in our lives with dignity, gratitude, and courage make us faithful servants of our Lord and wonderful role models for the generations to follow. ‡ [SCE]

# TAKE TIME TO BE HOLY

*Take time to be holy, speak oft with thy Lord;*
*Abide in Him always, and feed on His Word.*
*Make friends of God's children, help those who are weak,*
*Forgetting in nothing His blessing to seek.*

*Take time to be holy, the world rushes on;*
*Spend much time in secret, with Jesus alone.*
*By looking to Jesus, like Him thou shalt be;*
*Thy friends in thy conduct His likeness shall see.*

*Take time to be holy, let Him be thy Guide;*
*And run not before Him, whatever betide.*
*In joy or in sorrow, still follow the Lord,*
*And, looking to Jesus, still trust in His Word.*

*Take time to be holy, be calm in thy soul,*
*Each thought and each motive beneath His control.*
*Thus led by His Spirit to fountains of love,*
*Thou soon shalt be fitted for service above.*
*(William D. Longstaff, 1882)*


*More holiness give me, more strivings within.*
*More patience in suffering, more sorrow for sin.*
*More faith in my Savior, more sense of His care.*
*More joy in His service, more purpose in prayer.*

*More gratitude give me, more trust in the Lord.*
*More zeal for His glory, more hope in His Word.*
*More tears for His sorrows, more pain at His grief.*
*More meekness in trial, more praise for relief.*

*More purity give me, more strength to o'ercome,*
*More freedom from earth-stains, more longings for home.*
*More fit for the kingdom, more useful I'd be,*
*More blessèd and holy, more, Savior, like Thee.*
*(Phyllip P. Bliss, 1873)*

*( I have included some favorite older hymns that coordinate with the units. If the hymn is*
*unfamiliar to you, you may log on to nethymnal.com to hear the hymn played and find out more*
*about the author.)*

# GROUP QUESTIONS

*1) What has made you decide to participate in this class on spiritual aging?*

*2) What are some of the things you do to hold back the tide of aging? How is it working?*

*3) How is the second half of your life different from the first half?*

*4) What are the attitudes of your community and church regarding the elderly? Have you experienced ageism?*

*5) How are the elderly portrayed in movies and television? Do these images inspire or threaten you?*

*6) What are some of the expectations you have for this stage of life? Fears? Goals?*

*7) How would you like to see your spiritual life grow during this time of life?*

# ADDITIONAL ACTIVITIES

1) **GROUP:** Hold a "graduation" ceremony or have a party to affirm your transition into elderhood. Recognize it as the beginning of a challenging adventure. Hand out certificates (may be downloaded from the website www.autumnsaints.com) and a little gift for the road ahead.

2) **GROUP MEMBER:** For one week list the things that confirm your graduation into elderhood. Remember to list not only the negative things, but the ways in which you have matured (i.e. more patient, less apt to fly off the handle, more compassionate, more informed, etc.)

3) **GROUP MEMBERS:** Bring a picture and tell the story of someone you think has aged well. Explain what you think is the reason for their success.

# RESOURCES

[Please note: while I have read many of the books, visited web sites, and viewed videos that I have listed as resources, I have not read, used or viewed them all. Some of them have been chosen from reviews and excerpts on Amazon.com, brief overviews online, and recommendations from friends. These books have been selected to cross denomination lines. Check the publisher to select those that would best serve your group. I hope you find them useful in your study of the subject. 📖 This symbol indicates that the book is reviewed in the book review section.]

## BOOKS:

Bianchi, Eugene C., *Aging as a Spiritual Journey*, Crossroad Publishing Company, NY 1982.

van Breemen, Peter, *Summoned at Every Age: Finding God in Later Years*, Ave Maria Press, Notre Dame, Indiana, 2005.

Fischer, Kathleen, *Winter Grace: Spirituality and Aging*, Upper Room Books, Nashville, TN, 1998.

Killinger, John, *Winter Soulstice, Celebrating the Spirituality of the Wisdom Years*, Crossroad Publishing Company, NY, 2005.

Nelson, Harold R., *Senior Spirituality, Awakening Your Spiritual Potential*, Chalice Press, Missouri, 2004.

Robb, Paul, *Passage through Mid-Life: A Spiritual Journey to Wholeness*, Ave Maria Press, Notre Dame, IN, 2005.

Rohr, Richard, *Falling Upward: A Spirituality for the Two Halves of Life*, Jossey-Bass, 2011.

Weiss, Robert S. and Bass, Scott A. *Challenges in the Third Age, Meaning and Purpose in Later Life*, Oxford University Press, 2002.

## WEB RESOURCES:

www.senioradultministry.com A great website with lots of information for seniors.
www.msnbc.com Has a series called *Aging in America* which is worth watching.
www.autumnsaints.com

## ARTICLES:

*What do you know about Aging? Facts and Fallicies*, http://extension.oregonstate.edu/fcd/aging/extpubs.php

## MOVIES:

There are many movies out there that have senior adult characters, but they are not always portrayed in a favorable light. The following website has films on aging that are more helpful. The films are available for rent and might make a nice movie social for your group.
www.filmmakers.com

*Jesus Christ is the same yesterday, today and forever.*

*Hebrews 13:8*

*CHAPTER* 2

# WHAT HAPPENS NOW?

KEY THOUGHT: **"Even cowards can endure hardship; only the brave can endure suspense" [Mignon McLaughlin]. Elderhood is a time filled with uncertainty. Nothing is as it was and the future is often unclear. Jesus is the one sure foundation, the same yesterday, today and forever.**

As we age we become aware that the world is not as secure as we once thought it was. In our younger or middle years we felt in control. We planned with a certainty that what we planned would happen. We were certain that real estate was a good investment and that when we needed money we would be able to sell it at a profit. We believed that our children would outlive us and that they would be near us to oversee our care as we become frail. We assumed our pensions and social security would be there to provide income. We assumed our investments would be profitable. We assumed if we took a modicum of care our bodies would wear well. We didn't trouble our minds with the difficulties that *could* happen, we just assumed they wouldn't and that all was right with our world. In our latter years we have had enough experience to know that not everything is "in the bag." Life can throw us many curves. This is not a modern occurrence. Life has always been more unpredictable than we would like to admit. This time in life often highlights where we have been placing our trust and when those things seem less secure we ask ourselves "What happens now?" Just like the disciples walking on the road to Emmaus who had their world turned upside down with uncertainty, we wonder where Jesus is now. And just like the disciples we open our eyes to find him present, next to us in the breaking of the bread.

# LESSON 2, DAY 1
## WHAT'S GOING ON?!

**GRACE:** *To see Jesus as he walks with us amid our displacement and uncertainties.*

**SCRIPTURE:** Luke 24:13-35

## MEDITATION QUESTIONS:

1) How had the disciples' lives changed in the last week? Put yourself in their place and describe the disappointment you might be feeling.

2) How did their grief and disappointment keep them from recognizing Jesus? Where was he?

3) How did the breaking of the bread help them recognize Jesus?

## FOR YOUR CONSIDERATION:

For these two men, life had fallen apart. They had such high hopes, but the man they had pinned those hopes on had just been hung on a tree in a cruel and obscene death. They were hurrying away from the scene not knowing what might happen. Would they be next? How could they pull their lives back together again when they were leaderless and their hope had died? Their minds were churning with doubts and questions. They were so consumed that they failed to recognize Jesus as he walked next to them. Jesus patiently explained all that had happened according to the scriptures. Even in the midst of this enlightening discussion they did not associate this teacher with their Teacher. Not until he broke bread with them. We too are often so surrounded with our uncertainty and fears that we fail to see the Master who is right next to us, assuring us of his presence, offering us clarity and understanding from scripture, and calling us to a meal at which he blesses and breaks the bread.

**FOR JOURNALING:** Are their times when you are so busy rehearsing your doubts, fears and uncertainties that you fail to see Jesus walking with you? Describe one such time.

_____

_____

_____

_____

_____

_____

_____

_____

_____

_____

_____

_____

_____

_____

_____

_____

_____

_____

_____

_____

_____

_____

_____

_____

_____

# LESSON 2, DAY 2
## AVOIDING HASTE

**GRACE:** *To avoid making hasty decisions based on fear and to do the simple "housekeeping" tasks at hand until God shows us the way.*

**SCRIPTURE:** Acts 1:1-26

## MEDITATION QUESTIONS:

1) What were Jesus' instructions to the disciples?

2) What were the things that he promised for the future?

3) What was their "housekeeping" task? How did they proceed to complete it?

## FOR YOUR CONSIDERATION:

When the bottom falls out of a carefully-laid plan, we are thrown into feelings of uncertainty. The disciples were overjoyed at the resurrection of Jesus, but now he is leaving to return to the Father— leaving them to await the coming of the Spirit. As humans it is often our tendency to hurry decisions. We long to fill the vacuum as soon as possible. It is really hard to sit in liminal space, not knowing what is ahead. Jesus, knowing this, cautions them not to act in haste but to wait until they had the Holy Spirit to guide them. But what can one do while waiting? The disciples gathered in a room, trying to process all that had happened to them—Jesus' death and resurrection, the betrayal and death of Judas and the ascension of Jesus. They joined in constant prayer. They attended to the task of replacing Judas. They dealt with the things at hand. They did not attempt to move forward until they were able to receive and discern the Spirit. Processing, discerning and waiting are hard work, but if one is patient, prayerful, and attending to the simple tasks at hand, God in his time and place will make the way known.

**FOR JOURNALING:** Describe a time when you unwisely moved in haste. What were the results? How might the circumstances benefited by prayer, patience and doing the tasks at hand?

_____

_____

_____

_____

_____

_____

_____

_____

_____

_____

_____

_____

_____

_____

_____

_____

_____

_____

_____

_____

_____

_____

# LESSON 2, DAY 3
## WRESTLING THE ANGEL

**GRACE:** *That I might "wrestle the angel," instead of giving in to impulse.*

**SCRIPTURE:** Genesis 32-33

## MEDITATION QUESTIONS:

1) Why might Jacob be uncertain about returning home?

2) What preparations did he make?

3) How did "wrestling with the angel" affect the outcome of the meeting with Esau?

## FOR YOUR CONSIDERATION:

Jacob's time with Laban had been laced with deceit, the same kind of deceit that had caused Jacob to leave home. He was uncertain about what awaited him. He knew that Esau had reason to hate him. He was likely walking into retribution. When he heard of the army that Esau was bringing he was terrified. He took pains to do all that he could to prepare. He divided his family and goods hoping to preserve at least half of them. He prayed asking God to save him, recalling God's promise to make his "descendents like the sand of the sea." And he spent the late night and early morning hours wrestling with the angel of God. Sound familiar? We often spend the early hours wrestling with God, asking for him to bless us, give us wisdom, to sustain us with courage and strength and to work his plans through us. And like Jacob the encounter changes us. We are not the same as we were. We may even walk with a limp. We may not be given a new name but we are given a new outlook and the things for which we prayed. To proceed impatiently on impulse is to court danger. To "wrestle with the angel" is to wait on God, to not settle for the easy answers, but to come out prepared in the Spirit for whatever comes.

**FOR JOURNALING:** Describe a time you have wrestled with God. What was the outcome?

_____

_____

_____

_____

_____

_____

_____

_____

_____

_____

_____

_____

_____

_____

_____

_____

_____

_____

_____

_____

_____

_____

_____

_____

# LESSON 2, DAY 4
## STEPPING INTO THE SEA

**GRACE:** *To step into the sea that will start us on a new journey.*

**SCRIPTURE:** Exodus 14:10-31

## MEDITATION QUESTIONS:

1) Why might the Jews prefer to stay in Egypt rather than face the desert? Describe their uncertainty and confusion.

2) What is the significance of the angel and the cloud moving between the Jews and the Egyptians?

3) Why are the Jews told to stay still? Why are they told to move?

## FOR YOUR CONSIDERATION:

Transition times are difficult! We are neither here nor there. We cannot go back and the way forward often seems impossible. The future looks too bleak! But the Lord has great things in store. Moses told the people to "stand firm and see the deliverance the Lord will bring you, you need only to be still." This stillness in not lack of activity, but rather an awareness of the presence of God, a trust in his deliverance, and a hope in a promised land. The Lord asked why the journey had stalled. Why are they crying out in fear? Move on! Take the next step. Get off the banks, stop looking behind. Look forward! See how the way is opening. The winds of God have blown the water to the sides and God has cleared a path that marks the way. They could not see the way ahead until they had stopped looking behind. It wasn't until the last watch of the night that the Lord finally threw the enemies into confusion and destroyed them all. For us, too, there is a long journey ahead and not everything is clear but faith calls us to remain centered in God, listen for his voice and keep stepping forward until the time when all enemies are destroyed.

**FOR JOURNALING:** What are some of the ways in which you try to stay with known and familiar rather than move forward into the unknown?

_____

_____

_____

_____

_____

_____

_____

_____

_____

_____

_____

_____

_____

_____

_____

_____

_____

_____

_____

_____

_____

_____

_____

_____

# LESSON 2, DAY 5
## A FIRM FOUNDATION

**GRACE:** *That I might have a firm foundation withstanding the storms of life.*

**SCRIPTURE:** Luke 6:46-49

## MEDITATION QUESTIONS:

1) What are the three things that make for a strong foundation?

2) What happens in the storms of life when one does not have the true foundation?

3) What happens to those with a sure foundation?

## FOR YOUR CONSIDERATION:

Jesus warns the disciples that in order to withstand the storms of life one must have a sure foundation built by coming to him, hearing his words and putting into practice what one has learned. If we have not come to him before, now is the time to place our trust in him. It is not enough to be familiar with his words. One must put those words into practice on a daily basis. As one does this, the foundation becomes stronger. Each time we trust, and find him to be faithful, we are encouraged and strengthened for the next upheaval. We know that while circumstances are uncertain and mostly out of our control we can count on the faithfulness of a loving God. Each generation finds the world changing more rapidly than the last. My dad thought for sure he would see the Lord's return because of all the upheaval he saw in his lifetime. I now find myself thinking the same thing. The world is torn by war. The natural disasters are increasing—tornados, earthquakes and tsunamis, and floods. The economic climate is in flux with the rich becoming richer and the poor, poorer. We are all in need of a sure foundation. That foundation can only be found in the Lord. Where are you standing?

**FOR JOURNALING:** What are the uncertainties that you are facing in your life? How does having a strong foundation help you deal with them?

_____

_____

_____

_____

_____

_____

_____

_____

_____

_____

_____

_____

_____

_____

_____

_____

_____

_____

_____

_____

_____

_____

_____

# A FINAL WORD—BE NOT ANXIOUS

*By Lou Brakeman*

Be not anxious about tomorrow, about what you shall eat, what you shall wear, where you will sleep. God will provide. Set your mind on higher things, take courage, trust in the Lord. Those are the words of wisdom that come first to mind from the Scripture. But the unrelenting violence that dominates the news tugs at my heart and mind. This is not the place to analyze the politics of the current situations. What I want to reflect on here are my feelings and what I have tried, with only limited success, to do about them. There are many situations where we feel alienation and pain about news of the day.  Anxiety is a common condition for any sensitive person who is aware of what is going on in the world. How to cope?

Tuning out all the noise, burying one's head in the sand, instead talking about current medications, visits to the malls, the latest episodes of one's favorite daytime soaps, is one option. That I consider to be irresponsible escapism. Even more dangerous these moves only bury the anxiety deeper. I tried to cut back on how much I viewed. I kept up with what was happening, but did not immerse myself. That is one way to keep anxiety in check.

Another way is to talk out what I see, feel and think about it. Articulating feelings helps reduce anxiety. Being quiet, focusing on a beautiful flower, tree, even a photograph, simply slow breathing, going on a walk help too. Reading a novel, or mystery, getting absorbed in something other than the anxiety producing events helps.

The most effective therapy is to take the anxiety to the Lord in prayer—to talk simply and candidly with God. "Lord, I am really torn up by all the violence, by the death of innocent children, by the hatred and suffering, the relentless violence. Speak to those responsible and move them to halt the violence. At least help me to understand your will, your voice, your plan. Bless all those who are suffering. Move us all through this difficult time, help me to endure."

Author and Episcopal priest Alan Jones tells us that as human beings we long for God. To long for grace in a painful world is natural for us. Another author reminds us that while we may despair at the pain, we are to wonder at the creativity of our God. He must be up to something. He can create something out of the chaos. God will provide. ‡ [LB]

# HOW FIRM A FOUNDATION

*How firm a foundation, ye saints of the Lord,*
*Is laid for your faith in His excellent Word!*
*What more can He say than to you He hath said,*
*You, who unto Jesus for refuge have fled?*

*In every condition, in sickness, in health;*
*In poverty's vale, or abounding in wealth;*
*At home and abroad, on the land, on the sea,*
*As thy days may demand, shall thy strength ever be.*

*Fear not, I am with thee, O be not dismayed,*
*For I am thy God and will still give thee aid;*
*I'll strengthen and help thee, and cause thee to stand*
*Upheld by My righteous, omnipotent hand.*

*When through the deep waters I call thee to go,*
*The rivers of woe shall not thee overflow;*
*For I will be with thee, thy troubles to bless,*
*And sanctify to thee thy deepest distress.*

*When through fiery trials thy pathways shall lie,*
*My grace, all sufficient, shall be thy supply;*
*The flame shall not hurt thee; I only design*
*Thy dross to consume, and thy gold to refine.*

*Even down to old age all My people shall prove*
*My sovereign, eternal, unchangeable love;*
*And when hoary hairs shall their temples adorn,*
*Like lambs they shall still in My bosom be borne.*

*The soul that on Jesus has leaned for repose,*
*I will not, I will not desert to its foes;*
*That soul, though all hell should endeavor to shake,*
*I'll never, no never, no never forsake.*

*("K" in John Rippon's Selection of Hymns" 1787)*

# GROUP QUESTIONS

1) *How is the ability to live with uncertainty and ambiguity a sign of spiritual maturity?*

2) *How does the mature willingness to live with uncertainty and ambiguity help you develop the ability to overcome disappointment and encourage a spirit of gratitude?*

3) *How does this kind of maturity help make life an adventure?*

4) *Share the story of someone you know who has the ability to live life open-handedly and with courage in the face of uncertainty.*

5) *What spiritual certainties can provide a foundation for living with everyday uncertainties?*

6) *How can remembering God's faithfulness in your earlier life help you calm your uncertainties now?*

# ADDITIONAL ACTIVITIES

1) **GROUP:** Using a daily newspaper, circle the articles that make you feel uncertain about the future. List exactly what the uncertainty is (i.e. shortage of oil making gas prices so high that I might not be able to drive to the doctor or store.) Think of a promise or verse of Scripture that counteracts the fear that this uncertainty brings.

2) **GROUP MEMBER:** Keep a running list of unexpected gifts from God that have met needs even before they were realized. Post it somewhere in a room that you use daily and read through it often.

3) **GROUP MEMBER:** Think of a special unexpected gift that you can give to someone (a visit, a lunch out, a ride to an appointment, etc.) that will reassure them that God can be trusted to provide for their needs in unexpected ways.

4) **GROUP:** Think of someone in your church community who lives alone. As a group clean the yard, do small household maintenance, paint, or fix meals for a week (be sensitive to any dietary restrictions).

5) **IT IS HIGHLY RECOMMENDED THAT YOUR GROUP WATCH "SCARRED BY STRUGGLE, TRANSFORMED BY HOPE" VIDEO. This video may be purchased from benetvision.com.**

# RESOURCES

[Please note: while I have read many of the books, visited websites, and viewed videos that I have listed as resources, I have not read, used or viewed them all. Some of them have been chosen from reviews and excerpts on Amazon.com, brief overviews online, and recommendations from friends. These books have been selected to cross denomination lines. Check the publisher to select those that would best serve your group. I hope you find them useful in your study of the subject. 📖 This symbol indicates that the book is reviewed in the book review section.]

## BOOKS:

Chittister, Joan, *Scarred by Struggle, Transformed by Hope*, Eerdmans Publishing Co., Grand Rapids, Michigan, 2003. This book is the recommended companion book for this unit of Autumn Saints.

Farrington, Debra K. *Hearing with the Heart, A Gentle Guide to Discerning God's Will for Your Life*, published by Jossey-Bass, 2003.

Smith, Carol Ann, *Moment by Moment, A Retreat in Everyday Life* Ave Maria Press, Notre Dame, Indiana,1993.

📖Wicks, Robert J., *Living Simply in an Anxious World*, Paulist Press, 1998.

## DEVOTIONALS:

Chambers, Oswald, *My Utmost for His Highest*, Dodd, Mead, and Co.,1935. (There are many updated versions of this. My copy is dog-eared from many times of using the materials.)

Lewis, C. S., *A Year with C. S. Lewis*, Harper Collins, New York, 2003.

Murray, Andrew, *The Andrew Murray Daily Reader in Today's Language*, Bethany House Publishers, 2005.

Nouwen, Henri J. M., *Bread for the Journey*, Harper Collins, New York, 1997.

*Sacred Space* A book that can be purchased from the www.sacredspace.ie website. A wonderful way to interact with scripture!

*Time With God*, The New Testament for Busy People, Word Publishing, 1991.

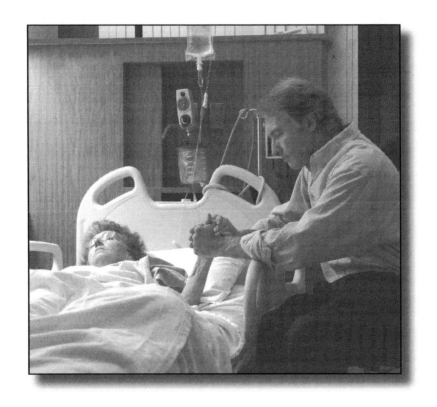

*Blessed is the man who makes the Lord his trust, who does not look
to the proud, to those who turn aside to false gods. Many, O my Lord
God, are the wonders you have done. The things you planned for
us no one can recount to you; were I to speak and tell of them they
would be too many to declare.*

*Psalm 40:4-5*

40

CHAPTER *3*

# MASTERING CHANGE

KEY THOUGHT: **Elderhood requires us to adjust to change —willed and unwilled. If we believe that God is in the change, we are able to transition to new life rather than simply endure or fight the change.**

Change comes to us all. Often it is a good thing that we are able to plan for, dream about, look forward to. But sometimes it comes unwilled and unwanted. It comes roaring through our lives bringing utter devastation in its wake. It can take the form of a natural disaster, death or illness of a loved one, economic loss, a physical disability, or a loss of identity. In our readings, Naomi has had a hard life, first leaving her homeland and then losing her husband and sons. Ruth too, is faced with loss and unwilled change. But she also *chooses* change as she decides to accompany Naomi back to her homeland. The Israelites experience change when they ask God for a king. Paul has radical change come into his life as he is knocked from his horse by Jesus on the road to Damascus. The newly born churches need to change as the Gospel is spread to the non-Jews by a man they formerly considered the enemy. No doubt you can think of times in your life when a change redirected and reshaped your life. Life was never the same after that change. In our earlier years much of our change is by choice. We chose to marry and have children. We chose a career. We seek a better job. As we move into elderhood many of the changes are unwilled. Middle-aged women ask each other "Have you started the change of life yet?" We often dread these changes. Others we fear. Some changes are a combination of both—willed and unwilled. We want our children to leave home and build an independent life but we also mourn their departure from the intimacy of our daily lives. To master change is a challenging part of elderhood. Only by seeing that God is in the change can we transition with grace.

# LESSON 3, DAY 1
## SOMETHING MUST CHANGE, BUT WHAT?

**GRACE:** *That I might be open to the leadership of the one true King.*

**SCRIPTURE:** 1 Samuel 8

## MEDITATION QUESTIONS:

1) What were the circumstances that led the Israelite to want a change in leadership? How did Samuel feel about this?

2) What was God's response to their request? How did he affirm Samuel?

3) What were the consequences in choosing a human king over God as their King?

## FOR YOUR CONSIDERATION:

There are times when the old no longer serves. Something must change. Samuel's sons were not following in their father's footsteps and their failure caused the Israelites to look for new leadership in the form of a king. God cautions them about the consequences of their choice, but allows them to move forward. Any change has implications for the future and it is best to know as much about those as possible before making any change. While we cannot anticipate every consequence of a choice, spending time with God will help us to discern the way. The Holy Spirit is within to counsel and guide us. Many older adults fail to be open to alternatives. They settle for the obvious default position of those around them. They fail to live with a sense of adventure. Sometimes God has a unique, off the wall, answer that can bless us and others in ways never imagined. As with the Israelites, he wants to be our King, and he will always open a way that is uniquely best for us. Of course like the Israelites we can insist on the way everyone else is doing it, missing the leading of the only true King.

**FOR JOURNALING:** What are some indications that things need to change? Are you open to the creative work of the King in your life? Why or why not?

_____

_____

_____

_____

_____

_____

_____

_____

_____

_____

_____

_____

_____

_____

_____

_____

_____

_____

_____

_____

_____

_____

_____

_____

_____

# LESSON 3, DAY 2
## ABOUT-FACE!

**GRACE:** *That I might be open to a change of direction in my life.*

**SCRIPTURE:** Acts 9:1-19

## MEDITATION QUESTIONS:

1) What was Paul's agenda as he traveled the road to Damascus?

2) How did seeing Jesus change that agenda?

3) What were the consequences of the new agenda?

## FOR YOUR CONSIDERATION:

There are biblical heros who encountered a mid- to latter-life correction. Moses was taken from his nomadic life and plunged into leading the Hebrews. The disciples turned from being fishermen, tax collectors, and rebels to followers of Jesus. Abram was told to leave his homeland and father a people as numerous as the stars. Paul was changed from a persecutor of the church to one who carried the Gospel to the Gentiles. The experiences of the first half of life uniquely prepared them for a later-life challenge. God does not consider the second half of life "down hill." For him the best is yet to be. These heros of the faith had eyes to see and ears to hear when God approached them. Paul was knocked from his horse. We too, may be knocked down in order to hear the voice of God calling us in new directions. This knock down may open our eyes to new avenues in which to serve God. Having cancer will put one in the mission field of those experiencing uncertainty, suffering and pain. This change pulls us from the comfort of our usual routine and gives us the opportunity to demonstrate faith to those who desperately need to know that God cares for them. Look for opportunity rather than bemoan the change. God has plans to bless you and others in the about-faces of life.

**FOR JOURNALING:** Are there ways that God has been calling you to a change of direction or agenda? What will you do about that?

_____

_____

_____

_____

_____

_____

_____

_____

_____

_____

_____

_____

_____

_____

_____

_____

_____

_____

_____

_____

_____

_____

_____

_____

# LESSON 3, DAY 3
## CALLED TO INNER CHANGE

**GRACE:** *That I might hear God calling me to inner change.*

**SCRIPTURE:** Acts 10

## MEDITATION QUESTIONS:

1) How is God preparing both Cornelius and Paul for their meeting?

2) What were Paul's prejudices that were being changed?

3) How did the overcoming of Peter's prejudices help him spread the good news?

## FOR YOUR CONSIDERATION :

Elderhood is a time of reflection. We look back to see how we have been shaped and who we have become. Sometimes we discover that the things and people who have shaped us have led us astray from God's will. Peter had been taught that non-Jews were unclean. They were not allowed to enter the inner courts of the temple and into the presence of God. Peter now learns that God does not show favoritism, but accepts all who fear him and do what is right. We may find that we have our own prejudices based on skin color, religious background, sexual orientation, financial status, or education among others. It is time to break down those barriers and recognize that God loves those we may have rejected. It is time for us to question our assumptions that those who are educated, rich, American (French, Hispanic, etc.), or of our own skin color are superior to any others. It is time for us to make those inner changes whether it be the prejudices we have mentioned, character defects we have acquired, or the failures to be all that God has called us to be. "Let us throw off everything that hinders and the sin that so easily entangles and let us run with perseverance the race marked out for us" (Heb. 12:1).

**FOR JOURNALING:** What are some prejudices, character defects or failures in spiritual discipline that God might be calling you to change at this time of your life?

_____

_____

_____

_____

_____

_____

_____

_____

_____

_____

_____

_____

_____

_____

_____

_____

_____

_____

_____

_____

_____

_____

_____

_____

_____

# LESSON 3, DAY 4
## CHANGE IN THE NAME OF LOVE

**GRACE:** *That I might accept unwilled change with grace and willed change in the name of love.*

**SCRIPTURE:** Ruth 1

## MEDITATION QUESTIONS:

1) What were the unwilled changes that had occurred in the lives of Naomi and her daughers-in-law? How had each responded to these?

2) What were the options open to these women? What did each decide?

3) How was Ruth's decision both courageous and loving?

## FOR YOUR CONSIDERATION:

Life had been difficult for these women. Unwilled losses had brought great change into their lives. Without men in their family they were no longer provided for or protected. In Ruth's time a married woman became committed to her husband's family. Ruth had done so and had grown to love her mother-in-law. When Naomi announces that she will return to her own country, Ruth makes the willed decision to go with her. God blesses her decision, and Ruth and Naomi find a place and someone to care for them. I don't imagine the adjustments were easy. Naomi was bitter and not an easy person to love, but Ruth remained a faithful daughter. Even willed changes can be difficult. Adjustments to new people, conditions and places take time. We often wonder if we made the right decision. We might even long for the past. However, if we make the changes as led by a loving God and remain faithful to him our willed and unwilled changes will be blessed in ways we cannot anticipate.

**FOR JOURNALING:** What has been the hardest unwilled change to make? Willed change?

_____

_____

_____

_____

_____

_____

_____

_____

_____

_____

_____

_____

_____

_____

_____

_____

_____

_____

_____

_____

_____

_____

# LESSON 3, DAY 5
## A FIRM PLACE TO STAND

**GRACE:** *That I might place my trust in a firm foundation, the Lord God Almighty.*

**SCRIPTURE:** Psalm 40

## MEDITATION QUESTIONS:

1) What are some indications that the writer of this Psalm might be in a tough spot?

2) What are the characteristics of God that David mentions as a basis for his trust?

3) How has the Lord answered his prayer in the past? How does David declare his trust?

## FOR YOUR CONSIDERATION:

David was in a time of change. He was on the run and his enemies were after him. He did not know what the next day held. David speaks of slimy pits and troubles without number that surround him, but he is placing his trust in the Lord to save him. It is easy for us to place our trust on less solid foundations, foundations that may give way. We often trust in our investments, social security and medicare, our community, our children, our doctors, or our church. If, however, we consider any of them our ultimate hope or security we are in danger. Any one of them may fail us in times of need. In times of change, only God is the sure foundation. "Many are the wonders you have done. The things you have planned for us no one can recount, they are too many to declare." Indeed God has given us a sure place to stand. "My hope is built on nothing less than Jesus' blood and righteousness; all other ground is sinking sand, all other ground is sinking sand."

**FOR JOURNALING:** How would you feel if your usual support systems were to fail—no investments, no health insurance, no community or church family? Would you have a place to stand?

_____

_____

_____

_____

_____

_____

_____

_____

_____

_____

_____

_____

_____

_____

_____

_____

_____

_____

_____

_____

_____

_____

_____

_____

_____

# A FINAL WORD—CHANGE & TRANSITION

In his book *Transitions: Making Sense of Life's Changes*, William Bridges makes the distinction between change and transition. "Change is situational. Transition, on the other hand, is psychological. It is not those events, but rather the inner reorientation and self-redefinition that you have to go through in order to incorporate any of those changes into your life. Without a transition, a change is just a rearrangement of the furniture. Unless transition happens, the change won't work, because it doesn't 'take'."

Twelve step groups talk about geographical changes. What they are referring to is that when situations are seemingly impossible, many people think that a new location, job, husband, etc. will make life better, but if the individual has not made the inner transitions necessary the problems follow them to the new location. The reality of the matter is that change happens. Sometimes a change is willed/planned and we set about to make it happen. We buy that condo, we move to Florida, we get that computer. Other times, it happens to us unwilled (not necessarily unwanted)—and we have made no plans for it to happen, it can happen slowly or "out of the blue." We lose our hearing, our only child dies, we inherit a property in the country, or fall and break a hip. Changes happen to all of us and it is how we accept and adjust to changes that help us in the aging process. Failure to make the transition, may leave us bitter and angry.

Many older people start to experience the changes that come with aging and think that a change of scene is the answer—moving in with the children, buying into that elegant retirement center, or going back to the home of our roots is the answer. In some cases that may work wonderfully well. In other cases, if the elders have not made a healthy personal transition to the changes happening in and to them, it may simply increase the stress.

The wonder of it all in the Christian life, is that every change (all things) can be used of God to transform us into the likeness of Christ. Everything can work for our good. God is present in all things and his love is constant. It is imperative that we seek him and allow him to oversee the journey from change to transition, if we hope to come out of change a new and better version of the self he created us to be. ‡ [SCE]

# YESTERDAY, TODAY, FOREVER

*O how sweet the glorious message simple faith may claim*
*Yesterday, today, forever Jesus is the same.*
*Still He loves to save the sinful, heal the sick and lame*
*Cheer the mourner, still the tempest, glory to His Name.*
**Refrain:** *Yesterday, today, forever, Jesus is the same.*
*All may change, but Jesus never! Glory to His Name!*
*Glory to His Name! Glory to His Name!*
*All may change, but Jesus never! Glory to His Name!*

*He, who was the Friend of sinners, seeks the lost one now*
*Sinner come, and at His footstool penitently bow*
*He Who said "I'll not condemn thee, go and sin no more,"*
*Speaks to thee that word of pardon as in days of yore.*
**Refrain**

*Oft on earth He healed the sufferer by His mighty hand*
*Still our sicknesses and sorrows go at His command*
*He who gave His healing virtue to a woman's touch*
*To the faith that claims His fullness still will give as much.*
**Refrain**

*As of old He walked to Emmaus, with them to abide*
*So through all life's way He walketh ever near our side*
*Soon again we shall behold Him, Hasten Lord the day*
*But twill still be this same Jesus as He went away.*
**Refrain**

*(Albert B. Simpson, 1890)*

# GROUP QUESTIONS

1) *Give some examples from your own life of willed and unwilled change. Which is easier?*

2) *What is the significance of being able to prepare for change?*

3) *Describe your comfort zone. What is it like to be pulled from that comfort zone?*

4) *What is the difference between being a resident and a pilgrim? What are some things that God allows that make us into spiritual pilgrims instead of lifetime residents satisfied with the status quo of this world?*

5) *Why do we resist change? Why is change harder as we grow older?*

6) *Is growth possible without change? How does willed change help us to mature? How does unwilled change help us to mature? In what ways do we mature? Do we ever stop maturing?*

# ADDITIONAL ACTIVITIES

**1) GROUP MEMBER:** Make an intentional decision to make some small change this week. Drive to church using a different route, sit in a different pew, talk to different people, eat a new food, read a book from a different genre, watch something totally new on TV, try a new restaurant, etc.

**2) GROUP MEMBER:** Look at pictures of yourself throughout the years. Look especially at the eyes and lines in your face. Make a note of the changes. Can you connect those changes with things that have happened in your life?

**3) GROUP:** As a group plan a willed change: choose a different place to meet (outside instead of in for example), plan a pot luck where members try out a new recipe to bring instead of bringing their old favorites, plan an activity with another denomination, ethnic group, or age grouping (children or youth.).

# RESOURCES

[Please note: while I have read many of the books, visited web sites, and viewed videos that I have listed as resources, I have not read, used or viewed them all. Some of them have been chosen from reviews and excerpts on Amazon.com, brief overviews online, and recommendations from friends. These books have been selected to cross denomination lines. Check the publisher to select those that would best serve your group. I hope you find them useful in your study of the subject. 📖 This symbol indicates that the book is reviewed in the book review section.]

## BOOKS:

📖Barnes, Craig, *When God Interrupts: Finding New Life Through Unwanted Change*, Downer's Grove, IL: IVP, 1996.

📖Bridges, William, *Transitions, Making Sense of Life's Changes*, Strategies for coping with the difficult, painful, and confusing times in your life. De Capo Press, MA, 2004.

Bridges, William, *the way of transition, embracing life's most difficult moments*, De Capo Press, MA, 2001.

📖Farrington, Debra K., *The Seasons of a Restless Heart, A Spiritual Companion for Living in Transition*, published by Jossey-Bass, 2005.

Ingram, Kristen Johnson, *Wine at the End of the Feast, Embracing Spiritual Change as You Age*, Loyola Press, Chicago, IL 2003.

## MOVIES:

*Shadowlands* starring Anthony Hopkins and Debra Winger. It is suggested that you watch this as a group and discuss the changes that occurred in Lewis's life and how they altered him as a person.

*Regarding Henry*, starring Harrison Ford. The story of a man who was a ruthless lawyer but after a shooting accident left him mentally incapacitated, changed his values and lifestyle.

*The Brides of Christ* is an Australian production. A group of nuns are facing the changes brought by Vatican II. The segment called "Ambrose" is especially touching in dealing with the emotional trauma of change. If you are Protestant do not be deterred by the setting!

## WEB RESOURCES:

http://www.blog.thirdage.com

This is kind of a fun website that has blogs from all kinds of people on all kinds of subjects regarding life in the third stage. You are welcome to add your own comments to those others have written. Some of the blogs have very practical and helpful information on changes and transitions.

*Do not store up for yourselves treasures on earth, where moth and rust destroy, and where thieves break in and steal. But store up for yourselves treasures in heaven, where moth and rust do not destroy, and where thieves do not break in and steal. For where your treasure is, there your heart will be also.*

*Matthew 6:19-20*

# CHAPTER *4*

# LESS IS MORE

KEY THOUGHT: **Downsizing helps us to simplify and become better stewards of what we own. It reminds us that that we are much more than what we own.**

Over the years we have been accumulating stuff—houses, cars, furnishings, clothing, memorabilia, collections, books, tools & utensils and much more! Often we have been defined by our stuff—an executive whose large home defines him a success, a woman whose closets filled with designer clothes define her a stylish beauty, or a hobbyist whose collections are a source of pride. As time passes it takes more and more effort to keep up with things. We find we have no more room to put things. We find it expensive to repair or replace things. We have things that are out-dated and even things we forget why we got in the first place. There are many things that contain treasured memories. The job of downsizing is difficult not just physically but emotionally. We could leave the job to our children but will they have the time and energy to distribute our goods or will they let everything go at a 10¢ yard sale? *Good stewardship demands that we responsibly distribute our goods to those who will benefit from their use.*

Not only do we need to consider what to do with our stuff, we need to evaluate our use of space. Do we still need a house with four bedrooms? Does it make sense to heat and air condition a large space when we only use an apartment-sized amount of space? For many it becomes a matter of income. As our incomes become smaller and fixed, a large mortgage payment may be out of the question and upkeep becomes impossible. For others the neighborhood is changing. Friends have left and the community has been redefined. All of these things make us consider downsizing and relocating. Much easier said than done. Starting over in a new place with fewer of our belongings around is not a simple transition. Downsizing and simplifying becomes one of the major tasks of elderhood. A task that reminds us that we are much more than a reflection of what we own.

# LESSON 4, DAY 1
## DOWNSIZING

**GRACE:** *That we may realize that more is not always better.*

**SCRIPTURE:** Judges 7:1-25

## MEDITATION QUESTIONS:

1) Why did God tell Gideon to downsize?

2) In what order did he downsize the men? What did he tell them to use for weapons?

3) How did God bring about the victory? How was it plain that it was God who won the battle for the Israelites?

## FOR YOUR CONSIDERATION:

Like Gideon, when challenge comes we gather all our resources. And like Gideon we think the more the better. But God tells Gideon he is over-resourced. If God were to allow this, the people would think that it was because of their resources that they won the day. Paul tells us that God's strength is made perfect in weakness. When the world sees victory in the midst of limitation, they know God is present. It is not our stuff that makes us strong. We will not overcome because we have more than the next guy. As we let go of the things that have given us a sense of security we become aware that it is God who is our real security and strength. We also become aware of our dependence on him. As we do this we are able to see the exceptional and unique ways in which he provides for us. Who in the world would have trumpets, clay jars and torches as weapons of choice! God's means are often so unusual that we know that only God could be behind them. As you downsize your resources, be prepared to see the ways in which God provides. Do not be afraid to let go of of your security blankets. God will give you victory over the enemies of life.

**FOR JOURNALING:** What are some of the "security blankets" to which you cling? What frightens you about letting them go?

_____

_____

_____

_____

_____

_____

_____

_____

_____

_____

_____

_____

_____

_____

_____

_____

_____

_____

_____

_____

_____

_____

_____

_____

_____

_____

_____

_____

# LESSON 4, DAY 2
## LESSONS FROM MANNA AND QUAIL

**GRACE:** *That I might realize that God provides for the day and that too much of a good thing spoils and steals from others.*

**SCRIPTURE:** Exodus 16

## MEDITATION QUESTIONS:

1) Why were the Israelites to depend on the daily provision of God?

2) How much were the people to gather? What was the benefit of this?

3) In our economic system, how does some having too much hinder others from not having enough?

## FOR YOUR CONSIDERATION:

God, through Moses, was using the time in the wilderness to create a unique people. A key quality of this "people" was that they were to depend on God to provide *daily*. He did not allow them to stockpile. They arose each day knowing that they could trust God to provide their needs for that day. Taking only what they needed for the day meant each person would have enough. We live in a day when stockpiling is considered a duty. We believe that it is our responsibility to have enough not only for today, but for the future. In this frame of mind, downsizing is a challenge. We hang on to what we no longer need simply because it feels safe. We keep things that could be beneficial to someone else. Living with only what we need gives us the opportunity to be generous so that others have what they need. Yes, we plan with intelligence, but we know ultimately that it is God who provides and he is to be trusted. This freedom of mind allows us to live simply and generously toward others.

**FOR JOURNALING:** What are the things that you really don't need that you continue to hold on to? Why do you do this? Are there those who could use what you no longer use?

_____

_____

_____

_____

_____

_____

_____

_____

_____

_____

_____

_____

_____

_____

_____

_____

_____

_____

_____

_____

_____

_____

# LESSON 4, DAY 3
## LETTING GO IS HARD TO DO.

**GRACE:** *To understand that our security and identity are not in things.*

**SCRIPTURE**: Matthew 19:16-30

## MEDITATION QUESTIONS:

1) How would you describe the young man who came to Jesus?

2) How is the young man's wealth a part of his identity?

3) Why did Jesus suggest that he sell all that he had?

## FOR YOUR CONSIDERATION:

We often associate people with what they own. "He's the man that drives the red mercedes." Or "She's the one with the Gucci bag." We believe that what we own says something about us. Owning much indicates hard work, cunning, intelligence, status, wealth, success. Owning little indicates poverty, need, bad-planning, laziness, lack of opportunity. While we may resent the stereotypes we tend to live by them. Because of this it is difficult to let go of the very things that give us indentity. Selling all and giving to the poor leaves us one of the poor. Like the young ruler many shake their heads and sadly go away. Keeping what we have gained, keeps our identity in place. Downsizing makes us confront how we feel about what we own. We may never give another dinner using our Spode china and sterling silver, but having it acknowledges that we could if we wanted to. Once it is gone we can't use its ownership as a feather in our cap. A four-bedroom house carries more weight than a studio apartment even if the apartment is easier to care for and all the space we really need. Jesus wants us to know that our identity is not in what we possess. We can let go of everything we own and still be a person of worth. Our worth is in the knowledge that God calls us his children.

**FOR JOURNALING:** What are the things in your home that will be the hardest to let go of because of what they say about you? That you are smart? Talented? Rich? Successful? Loved?

_____

_____

_____

_____

_____

_____

_____

_____

_____

_____

_____

_____

_____

_____

_____

_____

_____

_____

_____

_____

_____

_____

_____

# LESSON 4, DAY 4
## TREASURES IN HEAVEN

**GRACE:** *To consciously discover ways to lay up treasure in heaven.*

**SCRIPTURE:** Matthew 6:19-24

## MEDITATION QUESTIONS:

1) What are some of the dangers in having your possessions as your treasure?

2) How might one store up treasure in heaven?

3) How might serving God and serving our earthly treasure conflict?

## FOR YOUR CONSIDERATION:

Taking care of our earthly treasure is a heavy and costly responsibility. Upkeep on the house alone takes hours of labor and stacks of money—a new roof and paint job, yardwork supplies, plumbing, heating and cooling and insurance. Our treasures are subject to decay, theft, and destruction. No matter how responsible in the care, we cannot take them with us when we die. They may be passed on to someone else, but they no longer have any meaning for us. Treasures that are laid up in heaven are not subject to destruction. The kindness and generosity we extend to others last forever. How often do we fail to extend this because the responsibility of earthly treasure takes so much time. "I can't right now, I have yard work to do, the car to wash, the windows to clean." Downsizing gives us the opportunity to lessen the call of our earthly treasure and opens us up to laying up treasure in heaven. This can be a very freeing experience. It is possible to re-evaluate and set new goals as we let go of old prisons of responsibility. If we are careful not to fill the all free space with selfish pursuits, we can be blessed and be a blessing to others in ways that surely please the Father.

**FOR JOURNALING:** How might you redirect your attention from treasures of this earth to treasures in heaven?

# LESSON 4, DAY 5
## DO NOT WORRY!

**GRACE:** *To develop an attitude of trust that is free from worry.*

**SCRIPTURE:** Matthew 6:25-34

## MEDITATION QUESTIONS:

1) Who runs after the things of this world?

2) Is Jesus speaking literally in this passage? Why or why not?

3) What should one do instead of worry?

## FOR YOUR CONSIDERATION:

This passage of scripture seems totally impractical to us. We cannot imagine not worrying about the things we need. Jesus is making a distinction between being fearful and trusting God for our resources. This passage does not suggest laziness or lack of responsibility. Basically he is saying that if we are pursuing the right things in life, the kingdom and his righteousness, God will make provision for our needs. Early in life it is often through the means of our employment and industriousness. As we age it is often through the love and generosity of others. As seniors this is often difficult to accept. We would much prefer to work for what we need. Or we would like to think that the savings from our employment will be enough to see us through. We like to pay as we go. God has placed us in community that is designed to be interdependent and often this is the way he provides for our needs. Sometimes, we would rather pay out our last dollar to a professional yardman, than have a brother and sister in Christ do it for nothing. As we learn to trust in his goodness we must not limit his means of provision. Indeed, we need not worry if our trust is in the Master. We do not need to grasp our possessions to us in fear that we might be without necessities if we let them go. We do not need to fear receiving the gifts of others in the love of Christ. It is his way.

**FOR JOURNALING:** In what ways is God providing for your needs? Are you able to let go of things? Are you able to receive the gifts of others?

_____

_____

_____

_____

_____

_____

_____

_____

_____

_____

_____

_____

_____

_____

_____

_____

_____

_____

_____

_____

_____

_____

_____

_____

_____

_____

_____

_____

_____

# A FINAL WORD—LETTING GO

Letting go in all its various forms has been a large part of my life. My first real experience was right after college when I entered the Peace Corps in Guatemala. I moved from middle class affluence, to living in an adobe hut with no running water and a wood-burning stove. Shopping was done at an open-air market once a week and groceries limited to what was in season. At first it was incredibly difficult. I found myself saying "I wish I had …" (you fill in the blank). Before long, I began to appreciate the simplicity, lack of stress, and time for friends and family. My return to the United States was a real "culture shock." But that experience was my first building block in the "less is more" mentality.

The second real experience came in a different form. After twenty-five years of marriage, I left with one suitcase filled with clothing and twenty-seven boxes filled with quilting supplies. I had to let go of my dream of a successful marriage, but as I sat alone in an apartment in Chicago with my stuff around me—it was enough. Those boxes contained my security and identity. I was a *quilter*. But less than a year later, God called me to lay the quilting aside to move in other directions. The pain of letting go of that identity was a pain equivalent to extended childbirth. I didn't know who I was without the quilting, but God taught me that I was more than a quilter.

The next step in the process, was a choice between returning to quilting as a business or ministry. Most of the reason I had quilted previously had to do with getting attention for something I was able to do well—pride and affirmation. As I struggled with this choice, I tried the "business thing," investing a lot of time and money, but never feeling confirmed in the decision. This was a decision I was forced to abandon because I ran out of money. But as I opened myself to the quilting as a gift of ministry, I was able to see the wisdom of God. The women I ministered to were able to build a loving community that continues to this day.

Downsizing again came in the form of leaving a large city apartment filled to the brim with things I had acquired since my divorce, to moving into an 8'x10' room at my elderly mother's home. Selling ¾ of my belongings before I left Chicago, I found that upon my arrival I would need to leave at least another ¾ of what I had packed and brought with me, stored in the garage. Once again I have come to realize how little of "my stuff" is actually necessary. I had thought there would be a time when I would have it all with me again. Since then I have learned that I have no desire for it and appreciate the simplicity of life without it. Through all these downsizings and changes, God has been teaching me an essential lesson, that as long as I have HIM, I can do without the rest. [SCE]

# TAKE THE WORLD, BUT GIVE ME JESUS

*Take the world, but give me Jesus—all its joys are but a name;*
*But his love abideth ever, Thru eternal years the same.*
**Refrain:** *O the height and depth of mercy! O the length and breadth of love!*
*O the fullness of redemption, Pledge of endless life above.*

*Take the world, but give me Jesus—Sweetest comfort of my soul.*
*With my Savior watching o're me, I can sing though billows roll.*
**Refrain**

*Take the world, but give me Jesus—Let me view his constant smile.*
*Then thruout my pilgrim journey Light will cheer me all the while.*
**Refrain**

*Take the world, but give me Jesus—In his cross my trust shall be.*
*Till, with clearer, brighter vision, Face to face my Lord I see.*
**Refrain**

*(Fanny Crosby, 1820-1920)*

# GROUP QUESTIONS

1) *How does our society encourage us to need stuff?*

2) *How is our economy geared to our need for stuff?*

3) *How much stress is added to your life in the challenge to care for, protect, and keep up with property?*

4) *What is the cost of having lots of possessions—both property and stuff?*

5) *Why do we fear letting go of stuff?*

6) *How is our security tied to our stuff?*

7) *What are the emotional needs that push you to want more stuff?*

8) *How could you begin to let go?*

## ADDITIONAL ACTIVITIES:

1) **GROUP:** Find someone among your acquaintance who is anticipating a downsizing move. Plan to help with the move. Do your best to make it a positive experience for all who participate, so that moving day becomes a good memory.

2) **GROUP MEMBER:** Look around your home and locate at least 5 things that you could begin to pass on to others now rather than later. Write or tell them about the significance the item has had for you and why you would like them to have it. Say a prayer of thankfulness that it has been a part of your life.

3) **GROUP MEMBER:** Find at least 10 things that you have had around your house "in case you might need it someday" and if you have not used it in the last year, pitch it or give it away.

4) **GROUP MEMBER:** Make a scrapbook with pictures of your 12 most valued possessions. Tell how you obtained the item, tell why it has such importance for you, or include an interesting family story where the item was an integral part of the story. Plan to leave the scrapbook to a family member who will share it with other family members when items are being distributed after your death.

# RESOURCES

[Please note: while I have read many of the books, visited web sites, and viewed videos that I have listed as resources, I have not read, used or viewed them all. Some of them have been chosen from reviews and excerpts on Amazon.com, brief overviews online, and recommendations from friends. These books have been selected to cross denomination lines. Check the publisher to select those that would best serve your group. I hope you find them useful in your study of the subject. 📖 This symbol indicates that the book is reviewed in the book review section.]

## BOOKS:

Castle, Fiona &Greenough, Jan, *Living Simply: Decluttering Your Heart and Home*, Kingsway, 2006.

Heim, Joanne, *Living Simply: Choosing Less in a World of More*, Multnomah Press, 2006.

St. James, Elaine, *Living the Simple Life: A Guide to Scaling Down and Enjoying More*, Hyperion, New York, 1996.

📖Rohr, Richard, *Simplicity: The Freedom of Letting Go*, New York: The Crossroads Publishing Company, 2003.

Tabb, Mark, *Living with Less: The Upside of Downsizing Your Life*, Broadman & Holman, 2006

## ARTICLES:

Benavente, Janet, *Avoid Some of the Pain of Downsizing*, Colorado State University Cooperative Extension, 2006, http://www.ext.colostate.edu/pubs/columnha/ha0601f.html

Cartmell, Connie, *Downsizing Your Life: Aging Brings Need for Less*, Marietta Times, Mariette Memorial Hospital, OH, http://www.mariettatimes.com/news/story/new11_1028200620744.asp

Price, Christine, Ohio State University Extension, *Tips on Downsizing: Moving from the Family Home*, 2005. http://ohioline.osu.edu

Walker, Ken, *Is Downsize the Right Size?* http://movingforseniors.com/images/reallife_pg1.jpg

## WEB RESOURCES:

**www.livingtransitions.com/articles** Educational Programs and Resources for Later Life Moves

"With weapons of righteousness in the right hand and in the left; through glory and dishonor, bad report and good report, genuine, yet regarded as imposters; known yet regarded as unknown; dying and yet we live on; beaten, and yet not killed; sorrowful yet always rejoicing; poor, yet making many rich, having nothing and yet possessing everything."                                        2 Corinthians 6:7-10

*CHAPTER 5*

# AT A LOSS

**KEY THOUGHT:** Loss is an integral part of growing older. Each loss teaches us that God is in the midst of loss and that he never fails us.

Loss comes in many forms each affecting us each in different ways. Some are so impacting that life is never the same after—the loss of a spouse, close friend, physical health, or occupation that gave us a sense of identity. Some are gradual losses like the loss of sight and hearing, the inability to learn new things easily, or belonging to a world that seems to have rushed beyond our ability to catch up. Some losses isolate us, like loosing the ability to drive or move about easily. Each loss makes life seem less predictable and sometimes it seems that just as we have adjusted to one loss another is added to it. How does one adjust to the loss of parents and the discovery that one is now the eldest in the family? How do parents adjust to adult children who have left home and no longer seem to need them? How do book lovers adjust to the realization that even with the best of glasses they can no longer clearly see the words on a page? How does the musician play when fingers no longer obey his commands? How does a non-driver get places when everyone around them seems so busy? How does one deal with multiple surgeries for body parts that have given out? Of course we do not all suffer every loss but each of us will encounter loss in some form. It is important to know how to address loss. We need to know how to accept and adapt when loss cannot be prevented. Paul says of himself and his followers: "With weapons of righteousness in the right hand and in the left; through glory and dishonor, bad report and good report, genuine, yet regarded as imposters; known yet regarded as unknown; dying and yet we live on; beaten, and yet not killed; sorrowful yet always rejoicing; poor, yet making many rich, having nothing and yet possessing everything." [2 Corinthians 6:7-10] Loss teaches us this truth, that even when it seems as though we have lost all, we still possess everything, for "nothing can separate us from the love of God in Christ Jesus."

# LESSON 5, DAY 1
## ACCEPTING LOSS

**GRACE:** *To accept physical diminishment.*

**SCRIPTURE:** 2 Corinthians 6:1-10

## MEDITATION QUESTIONS:

1) What are some of the physical hardships that Paul endured?

2) What are some of the emotional hardships that Paul encountered?

3) How has Paul opened his heart to the Corinthians and what does he want from them?

## FOR YOUR CONSIDERATION:

Paul is willing to suffer all things if it will help the Corinthians to appreciate the value of what they have been given—the kingdom of God. He believes that the way he confronts the losses is a testament to his love for them and the power of the gospel. Although it seems that everything has been taken from him, he knows that he still possesses everything—the love of God in Christ Jesus. Paul mentions all kinds of loss: sorrows, distresses, difficulties, physical abuse, sleepless nights, imprisonment, public disgrace, misunderstanding, and near death. We know that Paul had a continuing "thorn in the flesh" which many believe was an eye disease that caused his eyes to run and impaired his ability to read and write. He is not addressing us from the sidelines. He knows whereof he speaks! It would be his desire for us as well, that we not throw away what we have been given by failing to see God in the midst of loss. Many are so overcome by the losses in later years that they focus only on the difficulties. They fail to see that God is releasing them from dependence on this life and this body and preparing them for new life and new bodies.

**FOR JOURNALING:** What are the losses you fear the most? How will the love of God and the hope of resurrected life help you deal with these losses?

_____

_____

_____

_____

_____

_____

_____

_____

_____

_____

_____

_____

_____

_____

_____

_____

_____

_____

_____

_____

_____

_____

_____

_____

_____

# LESSON 5, DAY 2
## ACCEPTING LIMITATIONS

**GRACE:** *To accept that our abilities and options may become more limited.*

**SCRIPTURE:** 2 Corinthians 12:1-10

## MEDITATION QUESTIONS:

1) What are some things about which Paul could boast?

2) How was Paul's thorn a leveling agent?

3) How is God's strength shown in Paul's weakness?

## FOR YOUR CONSIDERATION:

Our society is consumed with the idea of being strong, independent, gifted, beautiful, talented, wise and experienced. We want people to envy us. We want to be one step ahead of others. We want our children in the gifted class. We want to have something to boast about and when we do we do not hold back. Aging becomes a leveling agent. We find that we have less we can boast about. Our physical beauty fades, our strength lessens and our body gives out, our mental abilities and memory lose their sharpness, our accomplishments have become history, and sometimes it takes all that we have simply to make it through a day. Yet it is during this time that we learn that we can do all things through Christ who strengthens us. No, we cannot do all that we used to do, but we can do all that we need to do, not because we are so wonderful, but because God give us the daily resources to live in his strength. He provides us with not only inner strength, but with the inner joy that helps us to find the wonderful, lovely, beautiful, precious things present in life now. His love shines through and others know that it is not we who accomplish, but God who sustains and blesses.

**FOR JOURNALING:** How might loss lead you to trust more on God than in yourself? Where do you feel weak? How does God's strength shine through your weakness?

_____

_____

_____

_____

_____

_____

_____

_____

_____

_____

_____

_____

_____

_____

_____

_____

_____

_____

_____

_____

_____

_____

_____

_____

_____

_____

# LESSON 5, DAY 3
## ACCEPTING AFFLICTIONS

**GRACE:** *To accept that our afflictions help us to witness to the overcoming power of Jesus Christ.*

**SCRIPTURE:** 1 Peter 4:12-19; Lamentations 3:1-24

## MEDITATION QUESTIONS:

1) What the afflictions mentioned in Lamentations that might apply to elderhood?

2) What was the truth that comforted the author? What was his plan of "action"?

3) According to Peter how should one suffer afflictions?

## FOR YOUR CONSIDERATION:

Afflictions are the annoying inconveniences that are a part of becoming old—the inability to climb a step stool to change the lightbulb, having to ask for a ride, no longer being able to eat a favorite food, or needing to wear a "depend." None of these is a life-threatening occurance but they are things that take some of the immediate joy out of daily life. They limit what some would call the "quality of life." It is easy to fall into a complaining or sour disposition. As these afflictions mount up they can rob us of our joy. Others easily tire of our complaining. Lamentations reminds us that the Lord's great love is new to us every morning. The Lord is our portion. It is as we wait on him for our courage, strength, good nature, and sense of humor that we are able to face life with enthusiasm and joy. These afflictions are a reminder that it is not in this life that we are to find our completion. Peter reminds us to commit ourselves to the Creator and continue to do good.

**FOR JOURNALING:** What are some of the afflictions that you are experiencing? What are some ways in which you can overcome the tendency to complain about the afflictions that come with aging?

# LESSON 5, DAY 4
## ACCEPTING PAIN

**GRACE:** *To accept aches and pain that come with diminishment of the body.*

**SCRIPTURE:** Isaiah 53

## MEDITATION QUESTIONS:

1) What are some of the ways in which Jesus suffered pain?

2) How did he handle this pain?

3) How does actual pain develop our appreciation of what Jesus suffered for us?

## FOR YOUR CONSIDERATION:

We are fortunate to live in a time when palliative medicine helps to lower the levels of pain that we need to endure. Yet with encroaching age there is a level of ache that comes with bones and muscles that are no longer as strong or well tuned as they once were. While medications may moderate pain they cannot take away all pain everytime. There is no great virtue in suffering pain simply to suffer. Scripture never suggests that we should inflict pain on ourselves or not take medication that might relieve us of that pain. How much medication is a decision that must be taken under the guidance of the Holy Spirit and your doctor. When we are not able to completely irradicate pain, it may be helpful to remind ourselves of the pain that Jesus suffered for us. It can build within us a sense of closeness to him and gratitude for what he suffered for us. We must remember that pain is only for a season and that we will one day be in a kingdom where pain is unknown. "He will wipe away every tear from their eyes. There will be no more death or mourning or crying or pain, for the old order has passed away." [Revelation 21:4]

**FOR JOURNALING:** How has physical pain impacted your life? What end-of-life decisions have you made regarding regulation of pain?

_____

_____

_____

_____

_____

_____

_____

_____

_____

_____

_____

_____

_____

_____

_____

_____

_____

_____

_____

_____

_____

_____

_____

_____

_____

_____

# LESSON 5, DAY 5
## MORE THAN CONQUERORS

**GRACE:** *To be conquerors through Jesus Christ as we face the losses of later life.*

**SCRIPTURE:** Romans 8:35-39

## MEDITATION QUESTIONS:

1) What are some things Paul mentions that one might think would undo us? Will they?

2) What are the things that Paul mentions that will not undo us?

3) What is it that makes us more than conquerors?

## FOR YOUR CONSIDERATION:

It is quite common to look to science, especially medical science to deal with losses in later life. We want to avoid the losses if at all possible. We do not want to be bald or wrinkled so we look for ointments to prevent the condition. We hope and even expect that medical research will find a cure for all diseases, and hopefully before we get any of them. Scripture often talks about cures, but just as often it talks about enduring and overcoming the hardships of life. We live in a world that has been corrupted by sin and its consequences. Not all of these will be removed before the Lord returns and scripture calls upon us to be more than conquerors in *this* life. There is nothing in all creation that can keep us from being a conqueror, nothing that can separate us from the love of God who will sustain us in all things. Let us face the challenges of later life with courage depending on the love of God to give us the inner strength not just to endure but to be overcomers.

**FOR JOURNALING:** How might loss lead you to trust more on God than in yourself? Where do you feel weak? How does God's strength shine through your weakness?

# A FINAL WORD—SIGHT WARP

*By Elizabeth Magarian*

From the earliest pages of the Bible we read about the consequences of poor eyes. When Isaac was old and his eyes too dim to see, his wife Rebekah and son Jacob deceived him to get the blessing intended for the older son Esau (Genesis 27:1). Jacob preferred Rachel with a beautiful face over her other sister Leah who had weak eyes (Genesis 29:17).

Paul compares seeing through a glass darkly with seeing face to face suggesting that the dark glass won't reveal the whole truth. In contrast the eyes of God see everyone clearly. God knows what is going on perfectly.

The loss of sight, then, has all sorts of consequences, from the way others relate to those with low vision to the limitations in the ability to perceive others through body language and appearance, to observe what is going on, to see beauty, and to learn visually—the method through which so much information is transmitted.

Thus vision loss brings a lot of frustration and dependence on others and on alternative methods of learning and doing even the most basic tasks. Memory and the other senses become more critical. A sense of gratitude for what you can do, for cheerfully offered random acts of kindness, and for the willingness of society and individuals to offer assistance becomes important.

I have retinitis pigmentosa, a disease which first shows itself with tunnel vision and night blindness and progresses to the loss of colors and central vision. My problem was first noted by roommates who wondered why I always bumped into things when they didn't think I was absent minded. The first suggestion was to tie sponges on the corners of my bed.

I became aware of invisible people, and was thought snooty for not responding to waves from across the street. My eyes remained beautiful, and most people either never realized or quickly forgot how little I could see. I started using a white cane to alert drivers that I might not see them. Work as a math professor became increasingly difficult until it seemed best to retire.

Eventually reading became impossible, leaving me without the ability to read music, an essential skill in the choirs I enjoyed. I could no longer find the streetlights. My major exercise and means of transportation, walking, became dangerous. I became more dependent on others, but found others remarkably willing to try to help me continue participating in the activities that had described my life. Talking books and even software to read the computer screen gave hope that I could continue having access to literature and written communication.

More and more I edged into variants of what I had done from the ways I decorated pottery to the choice of knitting patterns to learning to improvise and play the piano by ear instead of only playing the classics I could read or had memorized.

In our society independence is so highly valued. Training in mobility, in ways to handle basic tasks, and in handling technologies that can help you communicate and access information can help maintain the ability to do things for yourself. Organization, keeping everything in its own place, becomes of paramount importance. Finding ways to handle frustration, perhaps through exercise, meditation, or some hobby like pottery or music that doesn't depend on sight, relaxing time with a friend, or even taking a nap when you feel accident prone or tired can bring back a sense of well being.

Increasingly, it is the inner compass that is needed both for orientation for walking and also to keep one's life moving in the right direction, which becomes the most important kind of sight. The confidence that a caring God is with us gives comfort and courage when frustration and challenge seem too great. ‡

# *OPEN MY EYES THAT I MAY SEE*

*Open my eyes, that I may see*
*Glimpses of truth Thou hast for me;*
*Place in my hands the wonderful key*
*That shall unclasp and set me free.*

## Refrain
*Silently now I wait for Thee,*
*Ready my God, Thy will to see,*
*Open my eyes, illumine me,*
*Spirit divine!*

(Clara H. Scott, 1841-97)

# GROUP QUESTIONS:

1) *Tell about someone you know who deals gracefully with tribulations. What do you think makes it possible for them to do so?*

2) *How necessary is acceptance to dealing with limitations? When do you accept and when do you fight against limitations?*

3) *How can one adapt to their limitations?*

4) *How important is community to living with limitations?*

5) *What are the most important tools to have in dealing with the limitations that come with aging?*

6) *Is it realistic to think that because you are a Christian and have lived a "good life" that you will be spared the difficulties of aging?*

7) *Discuss the climate of denial that exists in our culture. How do people think they can halt the aging process?*

8) *I once heard an older TV star say that as she aged she found that she was overly self-protective (I shouldn't use the stairs, I might fall etc.) and found she was loosing skills simply because she was afraid of what might happen. Have you found yourself doing this? What kind of things can one do to be proactive?*

# ADDITIONAL ACTIVITIES

1) **GROUP MEMBER:** Make an effort to find someone who has successfully dealt with the kinds of loss you fear. Ask them how they have overcome their fears and met the challenge.

2) **GROUP MEMBER:** Honestly journal a loss you have experienced. Don't hold back, make it an honest lament. Read it aloud to someone you trust. Burn the written lament and send it to God asking for his healing.

3) **GROUP MEMBER:** Find a way to serve those who are experiencing loss. Ask them what would be meaningful to them. Serve them as you would want to be served if you experienced the same loss.

4) **GROUP:** Make a list of losses that you fear and discuss how you might deal with them. Role play several of the losses which are most common to the whole group. (ie. The loss of the ability to drive.)

# RESOURCES

[Please note: while I have read many of the books, visited web sites, and viewed videos that I have listed as resources, I have not read, used or viewed them all. Some of them have been chosen from reviews and excerpts on Amazon.com, brief overviews online, and recommendations from friends. These books have been selected to cross denomination lines. Check the publisher to select those that would best serve your group. I hope you find them useful in your study of the subject. 📖 This symbol indicates that the book is reviewed in the book review section.]

## BOOKS:

Jacobsen, Fay W., Kindlen, Margaret, and Shoemark, Allison, *Living Through Loss: A Training Guide for Those Supporting People Facing Loss*, Jessica Kingsley Publishers LTYD, London, 1997.

Lewis, C. S., *A Grief Observed*, HarperSanFrancisco, 1961 (restored1996).

Ritter, Rick MSW, ACSW, CSW, CT, CFS, *Coping with Physical Loss and Disability: A Workbook,* Loving Healing Press, 2008.

Sitter, Jerry, *A Grace Disguised*, Zondervan Press, Revised edition 2004.

Sullender, R. Scott, *Losses in Later Life: A New Way of Walking with God*, Hayworth Press, 1999.

📖Viorst, Judith, *Necessary Losses*, The Free Press, a division of Simon & Schuster Inc., New York, 2002.

## ARTICLES AND SERMONS:

*Loss and Grief in Later Life*, PNW 439, November 2004, Oregon State University, a Northwest Extension publication. This is available at: http://extension.oregonstate.edu/fcd/aging/extpubs.php

*Coping with Your Loss and Grief*, PNW 438, 1993. Oregon State University, a Northwest Extension publication. This is available at: http://extension.oregonstate.edu/fcd/aging/extpubs.php
[Note: These two publications from PNW can be purchased for group use at a very nominal cost per brochure.]

## MOVIES:

*Treasure in the Darkness, Joni's Story*, a Day of Discovery Program.

If I say "Surely the darkness will hide me and the light become night around me," even the darkness will not be dark to you; the night will shine like the day, for darkness is as light to you.

*Psalm 139:11, 12*

CHAPTER *6*

# NOT AFRAID OF THE DARK

**KEY THOUGHT: There are times when all seems dark around us but the darkness is not dark to God. Even when we are unaware of his presence, he is still our Father working all things together for good.**

I don't understand. It doesn't make any sense.The way seems so dark. Where is God? He seems so far away!" Many of us think we would have much less trouble facing struggle if we understood—if we could pin down the "Why?" of it. Or, if we knew what the outcome of it was going to be. However, that would not  be living the life of faith to which God has called us. Scriptures are filled with lament, but they are also filled with the command to "fear not." With the maturity of spiritual aging comes the ability to live with ambiguity—the letting go of the need to have all the answers. The ability to know of God's continuing presence, love and providence even when we cannot feel or see the evidence of it. Hebrews 11:39 says "Not one of these people, even though their lives of faith were exemplary, got their hands on what was promised. God had a better plan for us; that their faith and our faith would come together to make one complete whole, their lives of faith not complete apart from ours" (Peterson, *The Message*) [and ours not complete without those that follow us]. Have faith, the story is still being written.

# LESSON 6, DAY 1
## JEREMIAH'S COMPLAINT

**GRACE:** *The freedom to express ourselves openly before God.*

**SCRIPTURE:** Jeremiah 12

## MEDITATION QUESTIONS:

1) What is Jeremiah's complaint? What is happening to Israel?

2) How is Jeremiah, a righteous man, suffering because of the evil of those around him?

3) What is God's promise for the future?

## FOR YOUR CONSIDERATION:

My grandmother used to have an expression about things "going to hell in a handbasket." I am not sure what exactly she meant by that, but I think that Jeremiah would agree with her saying in regard to his own times and people. People are telling him that God does not see or care about what is happening to them. It is possible that the elderly might think that everything is falling apart in the world and in their personal space. It is a temptation to think that God does not see, hear, nor does he care what is happening. We think that if God were at the top of his game he would do something to end war, bring our economy into some semblance of stability and balance, create just and merciful leaders throughout the world, help our youth find purpose and direction, and so forth. And because we do not see our expectations met, we wonder where he is. Is he asleep? Does he care? Psalm 121:3-5a "He will not let your foot slip—he who watches over you will not slumber; indeed, he who watches over Israel (and us) will neither slumber nor sleep. The Lord watches over you—." Regardless of how it may appear, God is present, caring and in control!

**FOR JOURNALING:** How might you be suffering because we live with evil in our midst? Does God ever seem indifferent or hidden to you?

# LESSON 6, DAY 2
## NOT SILENCED BY THE DARKNESS

**GRACE:** *To express rather than internalize our distress at God's apparent absence.*

**SCRIPTURE:** Job 23

## MEDITATION QUESTIONS:

1) What is Job's situation? What is his complaint?

2) How does he express the absence of God?

3) What is Job's weapon against the darkness?

## FOR YOUR CONSIDERATION:

Job has experienced many trials—material loss, loss of family and the loss of the sense of God's presence, perhaps the most serious loss of all. Job is unable to find God, yet he states *"But he knows the way I take."* We may not see God but he sees us. He knows what is going on. Even with all that is going on in Job's life, and even when he does not "see" God, Job continues to talk to God, believing that God hears him. Job's dialogue is not so that God will know what is going on in Job's life, it is so that Job can continue a relationship that now must be based in faith. We are so used to feeling God's presence and receiving his blessings that when they are withdrawn we feel lost. We wonder where God has gone and like Job cannot find him east, west, north or south. It is important the we, like Job, continue talking with God. We must express our faith that God is reliable. We must know that he is present even if we do not feel or see him. Job has expressed his hope in the midst of darkness (Job 19:25-27) and will continue to do so. "I know that my Redeemer lives, and that in the end he will stand upon the earth. And after my skin has been destroyed, yet in my flesh I will see God. *I myself will see him with my own eyes—I, and not another. How my heart yearns within me!*" Amen.

**FOR JOURNALING:** Make a list of your favorite verses that will sustain you when things are dark. Memorize one or two today.

# LESSON 6, DAY 3
## FORSAKEN

**GRACE:** *We ask for strength to endure the times when we are forsaken.*

**SCRIPTURE:** Matthew 27:45-46

## MEDITATION QUESTIONS:

1) Look back in this chapter. What has gone before this statement?

2) What aspects of the human condition did Jesus experience?

3) How did Jesus experience being forsaken? Do you think that he was forsaken or only felt forsaken? Explain your point of view. (There is no definitive answer.)

## FOR YOUR CONSIDERATION:

The book of Hebrews tells us that Jesus was tempted (tried) in all the ways that humans are tempted and tried in their lives throughout history. This is the basis of Jesus' understanding, compassion and prayerful interceding on our behalf. There are times when a person feels totally forsaken. Sometimes being forsaken is a reality. People *have* left and there is no one to take their place. People *are* abandoned. At other times people *feel* forsaken when in reality others are working on their behalf behind the scenes unknown to the individual. "Here we see Jesus plumbing the uttermost depths of the human situation, so that there might be no place that we might go where he has not been before."[William Barclay] Abandonment raises emotions of fear, anger, hatred, rejection, hopelessness, and resentment. Knowing that Jesus has promised never to forsake us can remind us that we may feel forsaken but in reality we are never alone. This helps us to overcome negative emotions.

**FOR JOURNALING:** Have you ever experienced abandonment as a reality? Have you ever felt forsaken? (Describe a time.) How might knowing that Jesus experienced this help you overcome such a situation?

# LESSON 6, DAY 4
## DARKNESS IS AS LIGHT TO YOU.

**GRACE:** *To know that God always sees us even in the black of night.*

**SCRIPTURE:** Psalm 139:7-12

## MEDITATION QUESTIONS:

1) Why might a person want to hide from God?

2) When might a person feel that reality is so dark that God cannot see him?

3) How is it a blessing to know that God can see in the dark?

## FOR YOUR CONSIDERATION:

The dark is scary. Just ask anyone who is awake in the wee hours of the morning. It is often in these hours that all our fears are magnified and our sense of being alone is heightened. We imagine all the evil that might be going on in the shadows. Our sins haunt us. We dwell on all the negative contingencies that plague life. We go over and over the choices we have made and the mistakes that changed our lives. The dark seems very dark indeed. But the dark is not dark to God. He sees us there in the dark. He brings his light into all the dark places. He assures us of his presence. He lets us know that he has plans for us—plans to prosper and bless us. He draws us from the dark into his light. We simply need to allow ourselves to be drawn. Sometimes we are committed to our negative selves and refuse to let go of our despair. We enjoy the rehearsal of it to others. But if we consent to let go of it, we can walk in the light as he is in the light. We can see life in all its abundance instead of death in all its darkness. It is a choice that we make.

**FOR JOURNALING:** What actions do you take that show you choose to walk in the light of God rather than in the darkness of this world?

_____

_____

_____

_____

_____

_____

_____

_____

_____

_____

_____

_____

_____

_____

_____

_____

_____

_____

_____

_____

_____

# LESSON 6, DAY 5
## *I WILL YET PRAISE HIM.*

**GRACE:** *To know that even when downcast a time is coming when you will praise God.*

**SCRIPTURE:** Psalm 42

## MEDITATION QUESTIONS:

1) What is the state of the psalmist's soul?

2) What is the psalmist's course of action when he is in this state?

3) What is his final word on the situation?

## FOR YOUR CONSIDERATION:

The psalmist knows that things are not as they used to be. He has fond memories of the joy of the Lord, but right now he feels downcast and alone. He wonders if this is the way things are meant to be. Is this all there is? The condition of his soul has affected his ability to eat. His enemies are mocking his faith, telling him that it is foolish to think that God will do anything. "Where is your God now?" they ask. The psalmist used to be one of the "pillars of the church"and it is assumed that one with such a position and reputation must be one of God's favorites. But, God is nowhere to be found! The psalmist pours out his frustration and his longing to once again be in the circle of God's presence—loved, cared for, appreciated. He is now called to demonstrate faith. It is easy to believe when all is going according to plan, when the evidence of God's love is plentiful. Can we still believe when life is filled with questions? The psalmist says that in spite of it all, he chooses to lay his distress aside and hope in God. He shouts out that in spite of it all there will come a time when he will once again praise God for all his benefits. What confident hope! Can we do the same?

**FOR JOURNALING:** What are the things that might keep you from feeling confident in God? Write a psalm that reflects your desire to trust God in spite of what is going on in your life.

_____

_____

_____

_____

_____

_____

_____

_____

_____

_____

_____

_____

_____

_____

_____

_____

_____

_____

_____

_____

_____

_____

_____

# A FINAL WORD—TURN ON THE LIGHT

The question is not whether or not there will be dark times, there will be. The question becomes: will the dark times overwhelm us or bring us to the light? One simply has to look at the news to know that darkness abounds. Children are abducted, drugs turn our youth into zombies and felons, families (Christian and not) break up at an alarming rate, homes are foreclosed, greed knows no bounds, partisan politics overrides the desire to serve the people, natural disasters leave people homeless and helpless. Indeed we can be easily be overcome with darkness. In a more personal way, darkness plays at the corner of our lives—the funds we worked so hard to accumulate are now worth less than we had thought they would be; our children divorce and move our grandchildren across the country; we become infirmed or frail, or our soul mate dies. We are teased with depression —to believe that all is hopeless, that the dark is all there is and God does not care. It is possible to reside in this darkness feeling angry, resentful, critical, and hopeless. It is tempting to rely on drugs to take off the edge. [Drugs may be an accepted part of medical treatment. But there are those who take drugs simply to escape the rigors of walking in faith.] We can abide in the darkness OR we can turn on the light of faith.

Psalm 139 assures us that this darkness is not dark to God. His light can overcome any darkness. Turning on the light is an action, a step of faith. It is choosing to believe like the psalmist that we will yet praise God. Maybe not this minute, this hour, or this day, but somewhere in the future we will once again see the Lord with our very own eyes. Walking in the light is taking the steps that are ours to take (maybe small ones at first), and moving forward running when we can run, walking when we can walk and standing firm when walking becomes impossible. Faith is believing that even if we have no understanding of why the darkness is present, there is One who does know and is in control. It is in knowing that perception is not everything. We may not feel God's presence, all may appear dark, it may seem that we are alone and forsaken but what is seen and felt is not the reality. Faith is a gift, but it is our choice whether or not to walk in it, to claim it when appearances tell us differently.

Why don't all come to the light? There are those who get mileage out of their difficulties. They thrive on the sympathy or extra attention. They may enjoy the freedom of having others take responsibility for them, (they fail to do what they are able to do to help themselves but instead manipulate others to take over), and they resist turning on the light when it might mean loosing the edge (control over others) that their difficulties have given them. A mother whose daughter comes daily to check on her after her surgery may not want to let go and release her daughter to weekly visits. It is a bigger temptation than we are aware of because to turn on the light takes effort, courage, determination, and in some cases even tolerating physical pain as we learn to redo physical tasks. And our efforts to move forward in faith might invite ridicule as others see us believing in a God who appears to be absent.

The call to walk in the light takes everything we have. We are often reminded in Scripture that we must not give in or give up. We must not let the darkness overtake us. We have one who is the Light of the World.

# THE LIGHT OF THE WORLD IS JESUS

*The whole world was lost, In the darkness of sin,*
*The Light of the world is Jesus!*
*Like sunshine at noonday, His glory shone in.*
*The Light of the world is Jesus!*
**Refrain:** *Come to the light, 'tis shining for thee;*
*Sweetly the light has dawned upon me.*
*Once I was blind, but now I can see:*
*The Light of the world is Jesus!*

*No darkness have we, Who in Jesus abide;*
*The Light of the world is Jesus!*
*We walk in the light, When we follow our Guide!*
*The Light of the world is Jesus!* **Refrain**

*Ye dwellers in darkness, With sin blinded eyes,*
*The Light of the world is Jesus!*
*Go, wash, at His bidding, And light will arise.*
*The Light of the world is Jesus!* **Refrain**

*No need of the sunlight, In Heaven we're told;*
*The Light of the world is Jesus!*
*The Lamb is the Light In the city of gold,*
*The Light of the world is Jesus!* **Refrain**

*(Phillip P. Bliss, 1875)*

## GROUP QUESTIONS

1) *What is the difference between spiritual darkness and depression? What are the symptoms of depression? What is the difference between sadness and depression?*

2) *What are positive action steps that we might take to lift the darkness/loneliness? What are the treatments for depression?*

3) *Talk about the ways society encourages us to deal with depression? Are these the same, different or compatable with scripture?*

4) *How are we dependent on our feelings when we think about God's absence or presence? Are feelings an accurate indicator of his presence or absence?*

5) *How does scripture serve us well in times of darkness and apparent aloneness? What is your favorite verse of encouragement in times of darkness?*

## ADDITIONAL ACTIVITIES

1) **GROUP:** Take a trust walk.* Ask the group about their comfort level during the walk? Were they relaxed? Did they see it as an adventure? Was there uncertainty or nervousness?

* A trust walk is where the members of the group are blindfolded. The leader leads them around the area as they hold hands. The group must trust the leader to give them safe instructions and lead them back to the meeting room unharmed.

2) **GROUP MEMBER:** Choose two unfamiliar verses that talk about God's presence in darkness and commit them to memory. If your memory is not particularly good, use calligraphy or fancy computer type and collage materials to make a picture to place in a prominent place and read it often.

3) **GROUP MEMBER:** If you keep a journal, read through the last year and make a chart of weeks. Give each week a title such as "optimistic" "down in the dumps" "hopeful" and see if there is a cycle or pattern. What might you do with what you have learned?

4) **GROUP MEMBERS:** Depression is a major problem in aging. According to Susan Sample at the University of Utah, 36% of older adults in outpatient clinics will be depressed, while 43% of older adults in inpatient clinics will be depressed and in nursing homes it can reach up to

51%. Suicide is more prevalent in those 65 and over than in any other age group. Take a screening test for depression: The Hamilton Depression Scale, The Beck Depression Inventory, or the Geriatric Depression Scale. If you score high for depression, contact your doctor and/or pastor.

## RESOURCES

[Please note: while I have read many of the books, visited web sites, and viewed videos that I have listed as resources, I have not read, used or viewed them all. Some of them have been chosen from reviews and excerpts on Amazon.com, brief overviews online, and recommendations from friends. These books have been selected to cross denomination lines. Check the publisher to select those that would best serve your group. I hope you find them useful in your study of the subject. 📖 This symbol indicates that the book is reviewed in the book review section.]

### BOOKS:

Lloyd-Jones, Dr. Martin, *Spiritual Depression: Its Causes and Cures*, Eerdmans, Grand Rapids, MI, 1996.

May, Gerald G., *The Dark Night of the Soul: A Psychiatrist Explores the Connection Between Darkness and Spiritual Growth*, HarperCollins, 2004.

St. John of the Cross, *Dark Night of the Soul*, Doubleday,1990.

Vanier, Jean, *Seeing Beyond Depression*, Paulist Press, 2001.

### WEB:

http://www.helpguide.org/mental/depression_elderly.htm

http://www.xenos.org/teachings/ot/psalms/gary/psalm42-1.htm

*Dark Clouds, Silver Linings*, Archibald D. Hart online edition
http://www.ccel.us/hart.toc.html

Come unto me all ye that are weary and burdened, and I will give you rest. Take my yoke upon you and learn from me, for I am gentle and humble in heart, and you will find rest for your souls. For my yoke is easy and my burden is light.

*Matthew 11:28-30*

CHAPTER *7*

# POWER OUTAGE

**KEY THOUGHT: Even when we ourselves feel vulnerable, unable to control and incapable of action, God is able to work all things together for our good.**

It is awful to feel vulnerable—without power to control a situation. I remember an experience when I had money in the bank but was told that I could not have access to it for weeks even though my deposit was a cashier's check. I went back to work very upset. My male boss who had an account at that bank, called in a favor and within minutes they released a significant part of the money. I was grateful but also very angry. It made me realize that a male authority figure had power to get what he wanted and I, a powerless woman, did not. I raged at the unfairness of it all. It opened up an awareness that I was very vulnerable to the whims of those in power. This is just one example of vulnerability. We may be at the mercy of a body that no longer works the way we want it to. We may become fearful when our minds no longer remember important things—like our children's names, or our own address or telephone numbers. We feel threatened when don't understand the language or terminology being used to describe a medical or economic procedure. We may decry changes that require us to do new things in new ways. It is difficult for many who need to move into their children's home where things are noisy and hectic, and where they have no participation in the decisions that affect the whole household, themselves included. What are we to do when we feel so helpless? We are to remember that God *is* in control. Even if we do not understand, he does. We are to remember his promises to care for us even when we cannot care for ourselves. We are to remember that he will never, never, never, never, ever forsake us!

# LESSON 7, DAY 1
## IN THE FACE OF DEATH

**GRACE:** *To recognize that corrupt bureaucratic systems and tyrants do not have the final word.*

**SCRIPTURE:** Esther 3:12-4:3

## MEDITATION QUESTIONS:

1) What was in the decree that made the Jews vulnerable?

2) Can you think of a more modern occurrence that makes this threat to the Jews more real and horrible to you?

3) How did the king demonstrate irresponsibility in this situation? In what other ways does irresponsibility make others vulnerable?

## FOR YOUR CONSIDERATION:

King Xerxes was known for his "great" parties. People were known to drink and carouse for days at one of his banquets. It is probable that disciplined and responsible leadership took a back seat. When Haman came to him with his idea to eradicate the Jews, Xerxes failed to check to see if the claims Haman made had any legitimacy. Money in the treasury sounded like a good thing no matter how it was gained. Recent history confirms that it is not unthinkable for corrupt persons to be filled with lust for power and goods. People are often at the mercy of such tyrants. Scripture does not promise that we will never be vulnerable. We may be placed in very difficult positions where we must face the possibility of harm. It is possible that corrupt bureaucrats may support war over the care of the elderly and poor. But like the Jews we can cry out to God knowing that he hears us. His plans for us may be difficult but they are always for ultimate good. We are not to deny our fears but bring them to God trusting that he cares for his people.

106

**FOR JOURNALING:** Have you ever been a victim of "the system"? How did you handle your vulnerability?

_____

_____

_____

_____

_____

_____

_____

_____

_____

_____

_____

_____

_____

_____

_____

_____

_____

_____

_____

_____

_____

_____

# LESSON 7, DAY 2
## IN THE FACE OF CENSURE

**GRACE:** *To have the faith and courage to do even the hard things.*

**SCRIPTURE:** Esther 4:4-17

## MEDITATION QUESTIONS:

1) What was Esther's first response to Mordecai's distress? In what ways do we try quick fixes?

2) How was Esther vulnerable? What would it take for her to appear before the king without being invited?

3) What was Mordecai's response to Esther's desire to opt out?

## FOR YOUR CONSIDERATION:

Esther felt that she could escape the decree of death by hiding out in the palace. Mordecai takes away her safety net by asking her to declare her solidarity with the Jews. He insisted that her very life's purpose was to appear unannounced before the king to plead their cause. This very act would point out the king's irresponsibility in allowing the decree in the first place. This was not an enviable position. It would take tremendous courage and faith to act on Mordecai's recommendation. She called upon the Lord as she and her entire household fasted. Esther was called to demonstrate her faith by accepting her vulnerable position but not allowing it to intimidate her. We are often called to demonstrate our faith in vulnerable positions. Like Esther there is no way that we can have success unless we go before the Lord with heartfelt calls for deliverance. We too must express our faith that God can work through our vulnerabilities. Paul states "Since I know it is all for Christ's good, I am quite content with my weaknesses and with insults, hardships, persecutions, and calamities. For when I am weak, then I am strong ( 2 Cor. 12:10 NLB).

**FOR JOURNALING:** Have you ever been asked by God to be in solidarity with those who are poor, sick, or distressed by actually being poor, sick or distressed? Have you thought that you might be placed there for "such a time as this"?

_____

_____

_____

_____

_____

_____

_____

_____

_____

_____

_____

_____

_____

_____

_____

_____

_____

_____

_____

_____

_____

_____

_____

_____

_____

# LESSON 7, DAY 3
## IN THE FACE OF RAGE

**GRACE:** *To know that the elderly are loved and protected by God even when others might find them annoying or expendable.*

**SCRIPTURE:** Esther 5:9-15

## MEDITATION QUESTIONS:

1) Why was Haman enraged?

2) What was his plan of action?

3) Relaying on past behavior, how do you think Mordecai behaved in the face of Haman's rage?

## FOR YOUR CONSIDERATION:

Anger is intimidating even for the most courageous of us. To know that someone wishes us ill creates an unsettled feeling at the very least. For example: There are those who are angry (who rage as Mordecai did about the Jews) that the elderly are taking from the system when they are seen to no longer contribute anything. They would say that our govenment has better places to put the budgeted money. There are even movements afoot to encourage assisted suicide when the elderly's quality of life is questionable and they are "costing more than they are worth." Some get quite heated; others are more subtle in their approach. We wonder if even those closest to us will resent having to use their resources to care for us when or if our own resources run out. In the face of this disregard, we must remember that God did not feel this way about the Jews and he does not feel that way about us. Our worth is not in what we can produce. We are valued because we are his children. We have worth as long as our lives have breath. He would not have us buy into this assessment of the elderly. He protected the Jews and he will protect us as well.

**FOR JOURNALING:** Do you believe that anger regarding the government money spent for care of the unprofitable elderly is justified? Discuss. How would you live in the face of this kind of anger?

_____

_____

_____

_____

_____

_____

_____

_____

_____

_____

_____

_____

_____

_____

_____

_____

_____

_____

_____

_____

_____

_____

_____

_____

# LESSON 7, DAY 4
## IN THE FACE OF ACCUSERS

**GRACE:** *To exude confidence in God's care as we age by remembering his past faithfulness.*

**SCRIPTURE :** Luke 23:1-25

## MEDITATION QUESTIONS:

1) Of what was Jesus being accused? How did Jesus respond to his accusers?

2) Did Pilate agree with the accusers? What was his point of view?

3) Why do you think that Pilate gave in to the accusers?

## FOR YOUR CONSIDERATION:

Jesus was accused of many things—i.e. instigating riots and setting up his own earthly kingdom, neither of which were true. He was able to stand quietly in the face of these accusations because he knew he was the Father's Son. In some countries the elderly are venerated. In our country they are often seen as a nuisance and given measly care and resources to get by on. There are those who resent the elderly and accuse them of taking up space and resources better used elsewhere. May we continue to fight for the dignity of *all* human beings. May we exemplify the attitude of Jesus toward the widows, poor and outcasts. And if we ourselves are ever placed in a position of the accused or disregarded, may we remember that Jesus cared enough to die for us. We are part of his family system, the body of Christ, set up to care for one another throughout *all* of life—sometimes givers, sometimes receivers. May we stand in the dignity of being the Father's child and a part of his caring family.

**FOR JOURNALING:** How will knowing that you are a child of the King help you in the face of spoken or unspoken accusations that you have outlived your worth? Might these accusations come from inside as well as outside?

_____

_____

_____

_____

_____

_____

_____

_____

_____

_____

_____

_____

_____

_____

_____

_____

_____

_____

_____

_____

_____

_____

_____

_____

# LESSON 7, DAY 5
## WHOM SHALL I FEAR?

**GRACE:** *To remain confident in the face of fear.*

**SCRIPTURE:** Psalm 27

## MEDITATION QUESTIONS:

1) Who are the enemies that conspire against the psalmist?

2) What is David's means of dealing with his fears?

3) What does it mean to "seek the Lord's face"? How does waiting on the Lord show confidence? How good are you at waiting?

## FOR YOUR CONSIDERATION:

David was in the presence of real enemies that were poised to attack and destroy his small army. Most elders are not about to be attacked by soldiers from an enemy camp. But elders are vulnerable to disease, frailty, economic loss, loneliness and isolation. Like the psalmist we must not let our vulnerability consume our thoughts or blind us to the beauty of the Lord. We must open our eyes to see the goodness of the Lord as manifested in the kindness and care of those around us, the beauty of his world, the availability of his own presence to comfort and guide us. We will be safe in his presence. Giving in to our fears makes it harder to wait upon the Lord. We may not always understand how the situation we are in works for good, but we do know that God is good and that he can see what we cannot. David tells us to be strong and take heart. Live in confidence. It is only by seeking God's face that we can overcome the sense of vulnerability that leads to anxious living. The Lord is my light and my salvation, whom shall I fear?

**FOR JOURNALING:** In what ways do you feel vulnerable? Has this led to anxious living? How does living in the presence of God lessen your sense of vulnerability?

_____

_____

_____

_____

_____

_____

_____

_____

_____

_____

_____

_____

_____

_____

_____

_____

_____

_____

_____

_____

_____

_____

_____

# A FINAL WORD—THE FACE OF GOD

*Psalms 27, 72*

Are we what we do? When we can no longer do are we worth less? Several years ago a famous London conductor and his wife entered a clinic and without ceremony ended their lives by injection. Their reasoning was that they were now a burden to their children and a drain on the system responsible for attending their infirmities. The news journal in which I read this article presented this as a noble act. For, is it not better to finish it all when our usefulness has ended and we require more than we can contribute?

Jesus began his Sermon on the Mount with the words, "Blessed are the poor, Blessed are the hungry, Blessed are they that mourn [who have lost everything], Blessed are those who are rejected and hated [and don't we reject being old, and the elderly as they remind us of our own destiny?] In other words, those on the very bottom of the rung are blessed. Our Psalm declares: "For he will deliver the needy who cry out, the afflicted who have no one to help. He will take pity on the weak and the needy and save the needy from death. He will rescue them from oppression and violence, *for precious is their blood in his sight.*" Jesus saw those at the bottom as having great worth not because of what they were able to do or produce, but because in them and for them he was able to do great things. Those who are healthy and active don't seem to need others to do for them—not even God! After all, they have it all together. They can do it themselves thank you very much! God is seldom seen or given any credit for what they accomplish.

It is in the poor that one may see the loving and compassionate care of God. It is in the old lady who embraces her poverty with a glowing sweetness and trust that one sees the provision of God. It is in those who have lost husbands and wives of many years and still continue on, that one sees the strength of God. It is in the lives of those who bravely face difficult treatments that one sees the courage of God. It is in those whose minds are fading that one sees the depth of God. When they have lost all else, they still remember "Amazing grace, how sweet the sound."

It may be true that our elders can no longer produce and that they cost us in dollars and cents. They also require an unselfishness that many are loathe to put forth. But, if we were to take these saints from our midst, where would we so plainly see the face of God?

116

# THE SERENITY PRAYER

*God grant me the serenity*
*to accept the things I cannot change,*
*courage to change the things I can,*
*and wisdom to know the difference.*
*Living one day at a time,*
*enjoying one moment at a time,*
*accepting hardships as a pathway to peace*
*taking, as Jesus did, this sinful world as it is,*
*not as I would have it,*
*trusting that You will make all things right*
*if I surrender to Your will.*
*So that I may be reasonably happy in this life*
*and supremely happy with You forever in the next.*
*Amen  (Rienhold Neibuhr)*

# GROUP QUESTIONS

1) *How important is power and control in our culture? Can you give some examples?*

2) *How do individualism and desire for control go hand in hand? Can you name some ways in which desire for control leads to a breakdown in community? [i.e. In today's family each member is likely to have their own TV so that they can control the remote and watch what they want to. How does this play out as we reach a time in life when we become dependent on others to help us meet our needs?]*

3) *How hard is it to fit into other's ways of doing things? [Think of an elderly woman who must go to live with her children.] What does it feel like?*

4) *What things might help us to adjust to lack of control and vulnerability?*

5) *How important is attitude in accepting lack of control?*

6) *How can courage be important in accepting lack of control? What is the difference between having courage and taking stupid risks?*

## ADDITIONAL ACTIVITIES

1) **GROUP MEMBER:** Think of the last committee meeting of which you were a part. Make a brief list of the issues to be decided. Think about your own need to have your ideas accepted. How did it feel when decision went in the opposite direction of your "wisdom" ?

2) **GROUP MEMBER:** For the coming week give up control of something once every day. Let your husband/wife/friend choose the place to eat, the program to watch, the movie to go to. Withhold your comments or suggestions. (Let your spouse use the romote for the evening if you are the one who usually has it nearby.) Calm your irritation with prayer.

3) **GROUP:** Role play the following situations.

   a) You go to get your license renewed and they tell you they must take away your license because your vision is inadequate.

   b) You are no longer able to go to your life long doctor because he is not on the insurance list of preferred physicians.

c) You are no longer able to eat your "normal" diet because of an illness, or because you have been placed in a nursing home with substandard food.

4) **GROUP MEMBER:** Invite your child or friend to make a meal or do a chore at your house as an experiment. Watch or help without making a suggestion or criticism. Was this hard for you? How did it make you feel?

## RESOURCES

[Please note: while I have read many of the books, visited web sites, and viewed videos that I have listed as resources, I have not read, used or viewed them all. Some of them have been chosen from reviews and excerpts on Amazon.com, brief overviews online, and recommendations from friends. These books have been selected to cross denomination lines. Check the publisher to select those that would best serve your group. I hope you find them useful in your study of the subject. ⬚ This symbol indicates that the book is reviewed in the book review section.]

### BOOKS AND ARTICLES:

Swindoll, Charles R., *Esther, A Woman of Strength and Dignity*, Word Publishing Co, Nashville, TN 1997.

Wangerin Jr., Walter, "Power in Powerlessness: Spiritual Mentors", *The Christian Century*, March 17,1993.

vonRosenberg, The Right Reverend Charles G., *"Strength in Powerlessness"*. A sermon given January 5, 2003 at St. Matthew's, Dayton, TN. This sermon may be found at http://www.etdiocese.net/sermons/2003/Jan-5-03-St_Matthew_Dayton.htm

### WEBSITES:

http://www.coping.org

This website has valuable information on coping with loss of control and letting go. Both sections have good checklists and advice to help with both of these difficult tasks.

Elijah came to a broom tree, sat down under it and prayed that he might die. "I have had enough Lord! Take my life I am no better than my ancestors." Then he lay down under the tree and fell asleep. . . And the word of the Lord came to him: "What are you doing here Elijah?

*I Kings 19:4-5, 9*

# CHAPTER 8

# ALL TIRED OUT!

**KEY THOUGHT: There comes a time when we cannot do those things that we have always done. Let us remember that we are not what we do, but who God calls us to be at every stage of our lives.**

I have a friend whose children refer to her as the "energizer bunny." For her eightieth birthday she went skydiving. Last year she did white water rafting and zip-lining across a canyon, but now at eight-three she finds it harder and harder to live up to their image of her. She tires more easily and it is harder to get from place to place. She does not want to let her children down but she realizes that she cannot go on this way forever! Her spirit is willing but her body is weakening. Aside from physical ailments, studies show additional reasons for exhaustion. 1) Negative emotions can make one feel tired: resentment, anger, and fear. 2) Everyone has experienced the depression, grief, and exhaustion that visit us after a traumatic loss. 3) We can experience *acedia*—a deadening to spiritual things, a boredom sometimes called the "noonday devil" for its appearance as the day wore on. (Also noted as life itself wears on.) We feel blah or "blue" and cannot really express why we feel that way but it colors everything we do. We let go of spiritual nurture because "we've heard it all before." It is chilling to note that suicide rates are highest in those (especially men) between the ages of 65-75. While other age groups may try it more often, elders who commit suicide mean to die rather than give a cry for help. Tiredness, exhaustion and depression are not to be ignored, but they are not a reason to automatically medicate with tranquilizers. Grief is a process that must be worked through. Negative emotions must be dealt with so that freedom from them may bring the joy of life back. Elderhood is a time of transitioning to new kinds of "spiritual work" that God brings to those who willing to transition from the old ways of doing to new ways of being. God has not abandoned us simply because we are tired or old. God has plans for us from the day of our birth to the day of our death. Let us not lose our spiritual zest along with our physical energy!

# LESSON 8, DAY 1
## BURNOUT—I'VE HAD ENOUGH!

**GRACE:** *To receive God's answer to the problem of burnout.*

**SCRIPTURE:** I Kings 19:1-18

## MEDITATION QUESTIONS:

1) What has caused Elijah to feel burnout?

2) What was Elijah's answer to his burnout?

3) What was God's answer to Elijah's burnout?

## FOR YOUR CONSIDERATION:

Elijah certainly has reasons to feel burned out. He had recently been through a very tough challenge with the enemies of God. We all know that great outlay of energy—even when we are relying on God's strength—results in a let down. We need time to let our body rest and to restoke our spiritual resources. But Elijah was experiencing more than this. At his weak point, he was being attacked and pursued. He is shaking with fear. He tells God that he "has had enough!" The angel of God ministered to his needs but did not allow him to curl up and die. God told him to get back up and face that from which he had fled. But he also reminded Elijah that while he felt as if he were the only servant of God there were in fact thousands of others who had also been faithful. God knew that a lone-wolf complex leads to a martyred sense of over-responsibility. To alleviate this he sends him to find Elisha who will be a disciple and fellow worker giving Elijah a mission and a partner. God recognizes that we tire and he ministers to our needs. He also knows the need for us to let go and commission others to carry the load. Elijah is to mentor Elisha until Elisha receives a double portion of the Spirit. When all is in place God takes Elijah home in his chariot of fire.

**FOR JOURNALING:** Are there younger people in your life whom God has called you to mentor? How might this address your sense of uselessness, loneliness, or vulnerability?

# LESSON 8, DAY 2
## EXHAUSTION AS AN ESCAPE

**GRACE:** *To learn to engage in prayer as an alternate to escapism.*

**SCRIPTURE:** Matthew 26:36-46

## MEDITATION QUESTIONS:

1) Why did the disciples sleep instead of watch and pray?

2) What were the consequences of sleeping when they should have been watching and praying?

3) How can an escape (whether sleep or mindless pastimes) be an unhealthy defense against facing the difficult?

## FOR YOUR CONSIDERATION:

It is true that the disciples had had a long and grueling day. They had been physically active and emotionally challenged. Jesus told them that the time was near when he must be lifted up to die. Jesus had talked about his resurrection, but the whole concept was beyond their ability to grasp. They knew that there were tough times ahead. Sometimes experiences like this seem just too hard to face. We too think that if we sleep we can wake in the morning to realize that it was all a bad dream. Jesus wanted his disciples to use the time to prepare themselves for the ordeal that they might resist temptation. But they slept and as a result gave in to temptation. They deserted Jesus. When we face difficult times we too face the temptation to give in to lethargy and escapism. Jesus calls upon us as well to prepare ourselves for our ordeals by prayer, watching and waiting to see the deliverance of the Lord. Do you use sleep as an escape? Awake, face life head on and use your time wisely to pray for strength and courage. Build your hope and trust in the Lord by recalling his promises. He will faithfully lead you through whatever challenges you.

**FOR JOURNALING:** Write about some time or situation when you have used sleep as an escape. Did it prepare you for your ordeal or simply eat up time? How might prayer have altered you or your situation?

_____

_____

_____

_____

_____

_____

_____

_____

_____

_____

_____

_____

_____

_____

_____

_____

_____

_____

_____

_____

_____

_____

# LESSON 8, DAY 3
## YOU CAN'T DO IT ALL.

**GRACE:** *To be willing to accept our limitations and receive help when needed.*

**SCRIPTURE:** Exodus 18

## MEDITATION QUESTIONS:

1) What was the situation? How was an outsider able to see it more clearly?

2) What was Jethro's answer to Moses' dilemma? What were the benefits of this solution?

3) How was Moses' humility demonstrated in this story?

## FOR YOUR CONSIDERATION:

Moses was exhausted. He could no longer do it all himself. He needed help. Humility is a rare commodity, but Moses demonstrated his, by accepting advice and help when he needed it. One of the hardest tasks for elders is to admit that we need help and that we can no longer manage it all ourselves. The tasks that we used to do energetically now tire us out just thinking about them. Our bodies simply cannot do what they would like. It takes humility to recognize and accept our limitations. And, it is especially hard to own up to our lack of energy and how tired it makes us to do things others seem to do with ease. Like Moses, the time has come to accept help. We must allow others to host the Christmas dinner, mow the yard, change the lightbulb, lead the small group. While we must not be slothful or take advantage of other's goodwill, there is no shame in asking or accepting help when needed and offered. Sharing the load develops and strengthens loving relationships. It allows others to share their gifts and to feel good about giving to us. Accepting help graciously makes for the loving, interdependent community that Jesus called the kingdom of God.

126

**FOR JOURNALING:** Are there times when you press yourself to exhaustion and pay the price? If so, why do you do this? How might accepting help from another help you both?

_____

_____

_____

_____

_____

_____

_____

_____

_____

_____

_____

_____

_____

_____

_____

_____

_____

_____

_____

_____

_____

_____

_____

# LESSON 8, DAY 4
## STRENGTH FOR THE WEARY

**GRACE:** *To draw our strength to run, walk and stand from God.*

**SCRIPTURE:** Isaiah 40:27-31

## MEDITATION QUESTIONS:

1) How is it helpful to know that the "Creator of the ends of the earth" never grows weary or tired?

2) How does hoping in God renew us?

3) Talk about times when you were able to run, walk or simply stand in his strength.

## FOR YOUR CONSIDERATION:

This familiar passage of scripture covers all the bases of a lifetime. There are times when we have felt the tremendous thrill of energy to run the race enthusiastically throwing out our arms with the joy of accomplishment. There are times when we have been able to walk faithfully through very difficult challenges resting in his provision of strength and courage. There are times when we have been able to do nothing but simply stand on his promises, bracing the wind and not giving in to defeat. It is a tremendous comfort to know that when we feel exhausted and barely able to stand that the Creator God is not tired. His understanding and compassion are beyond our understanding and his provision is constant and perfect. Whether we run, walk, or stand he is with us and he supplies the specific quality needed to stay the course. Trusting in him we are promised that we will not grow so weary and faint-hearted that we fail to complete our journey. His support can be depended upon. "Do you not know, have you not heard, the Lord is an everlasting God!"

**FOR JOURNALING:** Describe a time when the Lord has given you the strength to run, walk, or stand. How does this memory help you to face the unknown future?

_____

_____

_____

_____

_____

_____

_____

_____

_____

_____

_____

_____

_____

_____

_____

_____

_____

_____

_____

_____

_____

_____

_____

_____

_____

# LESSON 8, DAY 5
## THE BURDEN IS LIGHT.

**GRACE:** *Not to carry more than the burden the Lord has given us.*

**SCRIPTURE:** Matthew 11:25-30.

## MEDITATION QUESTIONS:

1) How was this message of Jesus in contrast to that of most of the religious people of his time?

2) How did Jesus' message give freedom and rest to the people?

3) How might our religious practice sometimes become a burden rather than a freedom?

## FOR YOUR CONSIDERATION:

Jewish religion in the time of Jesus was all about fufilling the law. The laws were filled with detail that affected every part of a religious person's life. The law required constant attention and created a burden that took the joy and freedom out of life. Jesus attempts to free them from this burden by telling them that his burden is light. He does not place on anyone more than they are able to handle. A key to overcoming exhaustion is not to place on ourselves more than what God is asking us to do. Just because we have done something for years does not mean that we are expected to do it forever. Perhaps we have years of serving the church and feel guilty just for thinking about letting go. It is important to ask if the things we do are what God is asking of us, or what we are requiring of ourselves. Jesus promises us that the burden he asks of us is light—to love God and others. He promises us help to carry the load. Do we do the things we do simply to be doing? Do we aim to justify our existence by what we do? Or are we following the plan that God has laid out for us—those "burdens" that allow for freedom and joy?

**FOR JOURNALING:** Are there responsibilities or obligations that you need to rethink at this time in your life? Are you experiencing the joy and freedom of Jesus' light burden? Why or why not?

_____

_____

_____

_____

_____

_____

_____

_____

_____

_____

_____

_____

_____

_____

_____

_____

_____

_____

_____

_____

_____

_____

_____

# A FINAL WORD—ARE YOU SLEEPING?

*Matthew 26:36-46*

An hour isn't much time. A single episode of a TV drama, a church service, a quick trip to the shopping mall, a typical college class all seem to happen in the blink of an eye. Not much time at all really. What was it that Jesus wanted his disciples to do with an hour? He wanted them to watch with him as his time of trial and death approached. Jesus knew that as he faced death, the disciples would be facing temptation. But instead of praying and watching with Jesus they fell asleep. They were tired, but perhaps like us they used sleep as an escape. The future was too sad, too painful and threatening to think about. Jesus was overwhelmed with sorrow to the point of death and still they slept. While they were sleeping Jesus prayed for an hour during which he asked to be spared the coming events, and as a result of this prayer he came to accept the will of the Father—a huge step forward from being at the point of spiritual death. He approaches the disciples once again saying that they must watch in order to be saved from the temptations that they will face and leaves once again to face his own temptations. Once again the disciples fall into sleep. Jesus, however, has prayed and is now ready to face what will befall him. "Rise, let us go." The disciples are physically refreshed but totally unprepared for what they will have to face.

What we have here is the difference between escaping and preparing. Our culture does not talk about real death. We love violence, but prefer it when our dead leap to life again to be seen in another episode. Hospitals, doctor's offices, and nursing homes are filled with the noise of innocuous television shows talking nonsense, because to their occupants, silence is unwanted. Facing our mortality threatens us. We too prefer escape. Jesus tells us this kind of escape is dangerous. We are missing the opportunity to prepare. Through prayer Jesus moved from terror to courage. We are growing old and death comes to us all. For Christians death should hold no fear. Yes the process itself is unknown and may be difficult as it was for Jesus. But we too can watch with him "one hour" and move from our fears to trust and dependence on the Father. We too can display faith and gain courage. What are you doing with your hour? Are you preparing or escaping? ‡ [SCE]

## GROUP QUESTIONS

1) *Why is burnout a common problem in our culture? What are the causes of exhaustion? How does it manifest itself? Is exhaustion a badge of honor that you wear demonstrating how busy you are?*

2) *Are you experiencing exhaustion as a part of aging? Describe your experience.*

3) *How do you deal with exhaustion? What are some ineffective means of dealing with exhaustion? What are the best "cures"?*

4) *How does getting alone with God help with exhaustion?*

5) *How does interdependence help prevent exhaustion?*

6) *Give some good suggestions for pacing yourself to avoid exhaustion.*

7)) *Why is it important to periodically evaluate the "to do" lists? Is everything you do worth doing?*

## ADDITIONAL ACTIVITIES

1) **GROUP MEMBER:** Make a list of small tasks around the house or at work that are not urgent but that you would like to see get done. The next time you feel "blue" do just one task even if you don't really feel like it.

2) **GROUP MEMBER:** Make a list of your favorite promises of God. List the times in the past that God has kept each promise. Read frequently to remind yourself of God's faithfulness.

3) **GROUP:** Select someone you know who might be depressed. Plan an activity that you know they have enjoyed in the past and include that person in your plans to experience that activity. (If you know the person likes to cook, plan a pot luck and ask them to bring a dish you have enjoyed in the past. If the person enjoys music, plan an outing to a concert. If the person likes the outdoors plan a picnic, etc.) The idea is not to "do for" but to elicit participation on an equal level.

4) **GROUP:** Design a faith walk of 6-7 stops for your church. After creating a spot of beauty, include a scripture and a book or plaque that contains church family faith stories that will encourage those who are flagging in spirit.

# RESOURCES

[Please note: while I have read many of the books, visited web sites, and viewed videos that I have listed as resources, I have not read, used or viewed them all. Some of them have been chosen from reviews and excerpts on Amazon.com, brief overviews online, and recommendations from friends. These books have been selected to cross denomination lines. Check the publisher to select those that would best serve your group. I hope you find them useful in your study of the subject. 📖 This symbol indicates that the book is reviewed in the book review section.]

## BOOKS:

Swindoll, Charles R., *Elijah, A Man of Heroism and Humility*, Word Publishing Co., Nashville, TN, 2000.

Weaver, Joanna, *Having a Mary Heart in a Martha World*, WaterBrook Press, Colorado Springs, 2005.

Weaver, Joanna, *Having a Mary Spirit*, WaterBrook Press, Colorado Springs, 2006.

## ARTICLES:
PHYSICAL TIREDNESS/FATIGUE

*Fatigue*, adapted from the pamphlet originally prepared for the Arthritis Foundation. Edited by Frederick A. Matsen III M.D, and Basia Belza, Ph.D, RN.

*How to Treat Chronic Fatigue*, http://www.australiandoctor.com.au/htt/pdf/AD_HTT_025_032___AUG26_05.pdf

Article on fatigue addressed to Doctors, but is interesting. http://www.orthop.washington.edu/uw/livingwith/tabID__3376/ItemID__85/PageID__111/Articles/Default.aspx

*Fatigue: Detailed Information*, Livestrong Foundation, http://www.livestrong.org/site/c.jvKZLbMRIsG/b.670127/k.A4B4/Fatigue_Detailed_Information.htm

*The Lived Experience of Feeling Very Tired: A Study Using the Parse Research Method*, Rosemarie Rizzo Parse, RN; PhD; FAAN.

SPIRITUAL TIREDNESS/ACEDIA

*Boredom*, Complete Book of Everyday Christianity, Intervarsity. http://www.ivmdl.org/cbec.cfm?study=105

Cutts, Jiko Linda, *Acedia and the Good Friend*, San Francisco Zen Center,

Wind Bell, Vol.34, No. 2 Spring/Summer 2000, pages 39-46.

deYoung, Revecca Konyndyk, *Resistance to the Demands of Love*, The Calvin Spark, Spring 2005. http://www.calvin.edu/publications/spark/2005/spring/sloth.htm

Funk, Mary Margaret, *Thoughts Matter*, Continuum International Publishing Group, New York, 1998, pp.93-110

Norris, Kathleen, *Acedia and Me*, Riverhead Books, 2008.

Williams, Rev. Bruce, *Apathy*, a talk presented on 10/22/01 at The Newman Center. http://falcon.fsc.edu/~bnogueira/apathy.htm

*I pray that out of his glorious riches he may strengthen you with power through his Spirit in your inner being, so that Christ may dwell in your hearts through faith. And I pray that you, being rooted and established in love, may have power together with all the saints, to grasp how wide and long and high and deep is the love of Christ, and to know this love that surpasses knowledge—that you may be filled to the measure of all the fullness of God.*

*Ephesians 3:16-19*

# CHAPTER *9*

# DEPENDENCE AS A GIFT

KEY THOUGHT: **Admitting that we need help with things that we used to do with ease is difficult. God has designed us to be receivers of other's gifts as well as giving out of our own resources.**

Our country is all about freedom and independence. We have taken it to the extreme. We now consider it abhorrent to need anyone or anything. We want to do it ourselves and when we can't we feel anger and resentment. We are envious of those who can. We fail to make our needs known because we do not want pity or others to think less of us. We are so desirous of our children's freedom that we push them away to do their own things and create a barrier of loneliness. This way of thinking is contrary to the kingdom of God. In God's kingdom everyone has a right to sit at the table, not just those who can contribute to the meal. God's kingdom is filled with love and generosity. We are continually told that we are to be *inter*dependent. There are times to give and times to receive. It is not a sin to be a receiver! We all love to give, but if everyone gives who is to receive? Giving often comes from pride. We feel in control. Receiving requires humility and honest admission that we do not have what we need unless we are helped by others. Many of us would rather sit in the dark than ask someone to fix the light. In addition, we need to rethink what we have to give. We may not have the ability to do or do for, but we have things that others are longing to have. We have encouragement, wisdom, great stories of God's faithfulness, gratitude, affirmation, and above all love. We have the wonderful opportunity to model how to grow old gracefully so that those coming after us will not fear or despise the aging process. We can show that we do not fear dying because we know that God has prepared a kingdom for us. Our hope, faith and trust in a loving God in situations that might daunt some, gives strength and courage to others. The currency may be different but in God's kingdom *all are givers* and *all are receivers*.

# LESSON 9, DAY 1
## PUTTING YOUR FEET UNDER THE TABLE

GRACE: *To accept the gifts of others.*

SCRIPTURE: 2 Samuel 9:1-12; 16:1-4; 19:24-30

## MEDITATION QUESTIONS:

1) Why did David reach out to Mephibosheth?

2) How was Mephibosheth betrayed?

3) What indicated that Mephibosheth cared more for the king than for riches and independence?

## FOR YOUR CONSIDERATION:

Even in our current culture, putting your feet under the table indicates acceptance by the host and an invitation to receive what he has prepared. In the story of Mephibosheth there is no indication that he is expected to return the hospitality. The host does expect a certain loyalty to the "family" but he understands the limitations that Mephibosheth brings to the table. David is the giver and Mephibosheth is the receiver. Ziba would have us believe that Mephibosheth only cares about what he is able to get. He tells David that Mephibosheth has given his loyalty to Absalom and hopes to secure his future even further. Mephibosheth reassures David that it is more important to be in community with the king than it is to receive independence and riches. He is comfortable putting his feet under David's table. In the kingdom of Jesus there is a very large table and all are invited to put their feet under the table. We are meant to receive from the king and from one another. It is a boisterous dinner filled with joy and laughter. Many refuse the invitation because they are determined to live on their own provision. Others refuse the invitation because they feel they have nothing to bring. Will you be there?

**FOR JOURNALING:** Are you able to receive as well as give? Give examples.

_____

_____

_____

_____

_____

_____

_____

_____

_____

_____

_____

_____

_____

_____

_____

_____

_____

_____

_____

_____

_____

_____

_____

# LESSON 9, DAY 2
## A COMMUNITY IN CHRIST

**GRACE:** *To receive as well as give.*

**SCRIPTURE:** Acts 4:32-37

## MEDITATION QUESTIONS:

1) What was the basis of the early church's generosity?

2) What was the community's attitude toward their possessions?

3) Who were the needy? How did this community rely not only on generosity but humility?

## FOR YOUR CONSIDERATION:

A unique quality of the Christian community was its love and generosity. In this community there were no needy people. We are amazed by the willingness of the participants to go so far as to sell their property in order that all might have their needs met. I am sure that the early church was not much different in its make up from many of ours. There were no doubt many poor, especially widows, who made up its core. The needy are drawn to the promises of Jesus to care for the sheep. These needy ones were able to admit their need and accept the help they needed from the generous. This type of community requires that we live in grace. We must understand that God is the source of all and that often he supplies our needs through the generosity of his other children. Some of us are like the story of the flood victims sitting on the roof, sending away the boat and helicopter waiting for God himself to save us. The humility to receive the provision of God through the hands of others, especially those who have sacrificed so that our needs might be met, takes a great deal of grace indeed! May God make us humble and able to accept the gifts of others as we give what we have to give.

140

**FOR JOURNALING:** Has anyone ever sacrificed (time, money, etc.) so that your needs were met? How did that make you feel? Did you have the grace to accept graciously?

_____

_____

_____

_____

_____

_____

_____

_____

_____

_____

_____

_____

_____

_____

_____

_____

_____

_____

_____

_____

_____

_____

# LESSON 9, DAY 3
## PART OF A FAMILY

**GRACE:** *To accept joyfully the interdependence of being family.*

**SCRIPTURE:** I Timothy 5:1-8

## MEDITATION QUESTIONS:

1) How does Timothy say that elders are to be treated?

2) How are the widows to be cared for?

3) What does Timothy say is the responsibility of the family toward its elders? How does this bring the life full circle?

## FOR YOUR CONSIDERATION:

Timothy is very strong on his position that the family must care for its own. Not to do so makes one worse than an unbeliever! He indicates that this is the way children are to repay their elders for the elders' care of them when they were young and unable to care for themselves. Life comes full circle. The family he refers to is not just the biological family but the church community as well. Visiting the homebound is a way of repaying their years of service—teaching Sunday school, gifts of hospitality, serving on committees, visiting the sick, and hours of prayer. To neglect our elderly members is a sin. The elders must recognize that this is a natural part of the cycle of life. It is the responsibility of the younger members to make sure the frail elderly are able to get to church for as long as they are able. We must be sure that their needs are met—daily necessities, yard work, home care, etc. And it is not just the tangible needs but the intangible as well. The needs for attention, recognition, appreciation, and love. The elderly must receive this care and attention with gracious humility and gratitude, giving what they have to give.

**FOR JOURNALING:** Who cares for the elders in your family? If you are an elder, who do you allow to care for you? Family or only those whom you have paid to do so? How do you feel about the need to depend on family? What would Timothy say about this?

# LESSON 9, DAY 4
## MUTUAL SUPPLYING OF NEEDS

**GRACE:** *To understand the principle of the equitable distribution of goods.*

**SCRIPTURE:** 2 Corinthians 8:10-15

## MEDITATION QUESTIONS:

1) How did Paul see equality?

2) Read the story from which he quoted. (Exodus 16)

3) What is the foundation principle that makes this equality work?

## FOR YOUR CONSIDERATION:

Paul repeats the lesson of Moses and the people of Israel—the equitable distribution of goods. This distribution is based on the foundation of the Father's ability to supply all our needs day by day. When we stockpile our goods for a rainy day fearing that our cupboards might be bare at some point in the future, we are showing our lack of faith. Moses told the people (as Paul tells the church) if everyone takes just what they need for the day, there will be enough for all. Our world has become unbalanced because of the greed of those for whom there is never enough. They always need a little (or a lot) more, bigger and better. We are to be good stewards and to do what we can as we are able, but we are to realize that the fruits of our labors are to be shared. If we have we give and if we need we receive without pride in the giving or guilt in the receiving. We assume that it is our responsibility to provide for the future. Instead it is our responsibility to be good stewards of what we have knowing that God will provide for our future. It may not be out of our own earnings, but it will be because we have been faithful day by day with what we have been given. We will have not too much—not too little.

**FOR JOURNALING:** In what ways are you curtailing your giving in order to provide for your own future? Does this reflect the lessons of these scriptures? How might you become a better giver or receiver?

# LESSON 9, DAY 5
## RECEIVING THE GIFTS OF SERVICE

**GRACE:** *To receive service to us as from the Lord.*

**SCRIPTURE:** John 13:1-17

## MEDITATION QUESTIONS:

1) Why did it shock the disciples that Jesus was washing their feet?

2) How did Jesus teach them both to receive and give service in this action?

3) How is receiving service vital to being able to give service? How does this work in day to day life?

## FOR YOUR CONSIDERATION:

Peter was shocked that Jesus would wash his feet. Jesus was the Master and Lord and should be receiving the service of others. Jesus shows that service is a part of what it means to be his disciple. Before they could give service to others they had to receive from him. We sometimes associate service with only the giving aspects. It is true that we must become servants. Jesus wanted them to know that they also needed to receive service. We receive the service of Jesus through others who wish to serve us in his name. When we reject their service we put ourselves above them. Saying we don't need their service shuts off the flow of love. However, mutual service keeps the love flowing one to the other. Peter wanted to cut off the flow by not allowing Jesus to serve him and we cut off the flow by not allowing others to serve us. We cannot be all taker, we must give. By the same token we cannot be all giver, we must receive as well. We want to give like for like, tit for tat. This is not the way Christian service works. We give what we have when we have as we receive what others have to give when it is needed. Times and gifts vary in the flow of life.

**FOR JOURNALING:** Describe a time when someone's service to you has changed your life.

_____

_____

_____

_____

_____

_____

_____

_____

_____

_____

_____

_____

_____

_____

_____

_____

_____

_____

_____

_____

_____

_____

_____

_____

_____

# A FINAL WORD—FEET UNDER THE TABLE

Make no mistake about it! Mephibosheth was in the very vulnerable and powerless condition that we have been discussing. He was limited both physically and financially. What would have come to him (the kingship and great wealth) was trashed by a mentally unbalanced grandfather (Saul) and given to someone outside the family. His father (Jonathan) was taken from him at a very early age. He was dependent on the "kindness of strangers" and lived in a town called Lo Debar (meaning no pasture or no promise). David's goodness to him was unexpected, undeserved and outstandingly generous! Mephibosheth was given fellowship at the king's table and independence and status in the form of wealth and lands.

Many sermons end here using this rightfully as an analogy for God's goodness to each of his undeserving children. However, Mephibosheth's story does not end here and it is important to follow it through to its completion in scripture. Mephibosheth was betrayed. The king was disturbed that Mephibosheth had not gone with him when he fled Jerusalem during his son's (Absalom's) coup. How could someone for whom David had done so much not support him in his own time of betrayal? Ziba had told David that Mephibosheth hoped to gain even more from Absalom's coup. Mephibosheth was devastated. He had not wanted his own handicap to be an additional handicap to David. In fact he showed all the signs of serious mourning for the misunderstanding. David took back part of his lands, perhaps not really sure whom to believe. Some have said that this was simply a test given to Mephibosheth. Mephibosheth makes a remarkable statement. Basically, he says that it is more important for him to be in fellowship with the king and those at his table, than it is for him to own property—the symbol of his earthly security, status, wealth and independence. In effect he was choosing dependence over independence.

I think of how often we choose to hold on to our pride and independence at all costs. We don't want to be a burden to anyone—so we become lonely, isolated, home-bound. Perhaps we don't want to ask for a ride someplace. We don't want to let someone see that we are no longer able to keep house as we used to so we don't let them in the door. We don't want to let anyone know that we are in pain and cannot afford our meds so we avoid situations where that pain might be evident. We can't afford to bring a dish to the potluck so we make excuses for not attending. We used to pride ourselves on our appearance, but now we think we look haggard, old, and cannot bear to have anyone see us like this. We fear others taking control and making decisions for us.

The king's table is waiting for us. Graciously he has seated people at his table who own cars, people who would love to get their hands on a dirty house and make it shine, people that would love to help with a garden, people who would love your presence even without a potluck dish. We all love to be givers, but whom do we give to if no one makes their needs known? One of the greatest gifts we can give is to be available to receive the gifts that others are longing to give! It is vital for us to be at the table. To be in fellowship. To be a part of the covenant family.

It is not only important to receive the gifts, it is also essential to receive the gifts graciously and with heartfelt thanksgiving. Solomon could have said in his Ecclesiastes passage—a time to give and a time to receive.

It is during these times of receiving that generativity happens. This is when we swap the stories of God's faithfulness. This is when we listen to the cries of the heart. This is when we can encourage and uplift those who are helping us. We can bless as we are blessed and it is not a one-way street after all! ‡ [SCE]

# GROUP QUESTIONS

1) *How do you think God meant his family to operate in terms of dependence, independence, and interdependence? What scripture can you use to back up your thoughts?*

2) *How might our fight for independence be a sin?*

3) *How does graceful acceptance of our situation free us to be lovingly open to the help of others?*

4) *Why do you think we fight so hard to maintain our independence and avoid dependence?*

5) *How do we give help and preserve the dignity of the person being helped?*

6) *A great deal of our shaping and learning comes from surviving challenging circumstances. Do you think it's possible that when we protect others from having to assume the difficult task of caring for us in our dependence, that we are actually blocking some important learning and shaping growth in their lives? Discuss.*

7) *Peter van Breemen in his book "Summoned at Every Age" says: "Every old person can end up facing the challenge of living one's dependence in such a way that it can become a gift to one's family and acquaintances." How do we receive help and make it a mutual blessing? How can it be like sitting at a family pot luck dinner?*

8) *Often times we "bank" our help so that when we are needful we think we deserve or are owed help (maybe from the same person we gave it to). God's plan for grace does not include keeping such accounts. What do you think he would say about such an attitude?*

9) *How do you think our culture's call to "provide for ourselves in our old age" might be seen in God's economy?*

10) *Tell a story about someone you know who exhibits grace-filled dependence.*

## ADDITIONAL ACTIVITIES

1) **GROUP MEMBER**: Pick one time during the week to ask for help when you would normally try to bluff not needing it. (i.e. Ask for directions *before* you get lost; Have someone help you lift that box *before* you put your back out, etc.). Share the experience with your group.

2) **GROUP:** Using a simple child's puzzle (100 pieces or less) give each group member some of the pieces. Work together to put the puzzle together. What would it be like if one of the group refused to let go of the pieces? What would it be like if one of the group refused to accept the pieces of the rest of the group?

3) **GROUP:** Plan some simple activities that might actually occur and role play:

a) Pretend someone has had a stoke and lost the use of their hands. Tie the hands behind the back and feed that person. Discuss the feelings (silly? frustrated?)

b) Blindfold one of your members, and try to describe a picture from a magazine so that that person can see in their mind's eye. For the hearing impaired: How might you help someone to hear what is going on?

## RESOURCES:

[Please note: while I have read many of the books, visited web sites, and viewed videos that I have listed as resources, I have not read, used or viewed them all. Some of them have been chosen from reviews and excerpts on Amazon.com, brief overviews online, and recommendations from friends. These books have been selected to cross denomination lines. Check the publisher to select those that would best serve your group. I hope you find them useful in your study of the subject. 📖 This symbol indicates that the book is reviewed in the book review section.

## BOOKS:

Sullender, R. Scott, *Losses in Later Life* (Especially chapter 5), Haworth Pastoral Press, New York, 1999.

📖vanBreemen, Peter, *Summoned at Every Age*, Ave Maria Press, 2005.

## SERMONS AND ARTICLES AVAILABLE ON LINE:

*Are You Handicapped?* http:/www.wholeperson-counseling.org/id/mephibosheth.html

*God's Perspective on Ministering to the Disabled,* http://www.gty.org/resources.php?section=transcripts&aid=231368

*His Restoration,* http://www.pbministries.org/books/pink/David/Vol2/david2_75.htm

*Mephibosheth and Me,* http://www.growingchristians.org/dfgc/mephibos.htm

## When Dependency Increases Series

Series Description: *When Dependency Increases* is a series of seven multi-media workshop designed for families, care providers, and older adults. Each workshop package includes a 16-20 minute color slide/tape production, script, a comprehensive instructor's guide for conducting a 1 to 3 hour workshop, overhead transparency masters, participant handouts, worksheets, and color videotape (of the slide/tape program).

The workshop is sold as a complete package (includes the videotape). The videotapes are not sold separately.

Publications under this series:

I - Best Wishes Edith and Henry! Program explores family relationships and decisions in later life. The story of Edith and Henry's family motivates viewers to consider the impact of decisions on everyone and to identify alternatives for resolving issues that are raised. Guidelines are presented which apply to nearly any decision families face when an older relative becomes dependent.

Publication Price : $ 50.00 each

II - 260 Primrose Lane Program explores living arrangement options and decisions in later life. Through the lives of Ethyl, Claire, Sara and Norman, viewers learn about the impact a change in living arrangements can have on the older person. Discussion focuses on living arrangement options and factors to consider in making housing choices.

Publication Price : $ 50.00 each

III - The Dollmaker Program focuses on the importance of caregivers taking care of themselves. The caregiver's health is at stake when Alyce provides 24 hour care for Ernie and refuses help and respite. Alyce becomes isolated and loses her health, relationships, and interest in life. Guidelines are suggested for making caregiving decisions and reducing caregiver stress.

Publication Price : $ 50.00 each

IV - Due Upon Receipt Program addresses the financial concerns in later life. Through the stories of Isabel, Carlos, Fred and Maggie and their families, viewers learn about problems low income elderly face, resources available, health insurance coverage, guardianship and conservatorship, nursing home costs, and the importance of family members talking together about financial concerns. Guidelines are presented for making financial decisions.

Publication Price : $ 50.00 each

V - The Second Story Program explores loss and grief in later life. Following the death of his wife, William Sanders, 70, tried to "be strong" and didn't talk about his wife's death. Six months later he experiences additional losses. Viewers learn about the grief process, the impact of multiple losses, and ways to support the bereaved.

Publication Price : $ 50.00 each

VI - The Final Course Program focuses on depression in later life. Mrs. Murphy, 72, took great pride in her roles as wife and mother and her ability to make the finest desserts. Following a mild stroke, she becomes depressed. Viewers learn about signs of depression and how they can help a depressed person.

Publication Price : $ 50.00 each

VII - Winter Comforts Program focuses on alcohol problems in later life. Following retirement, Phyllis' one glass of wine gradually extends to several glasses to "drive away the loneliness." She becomes forgetful, develops unexplained bruises, calls at odd hours, and exhibits behavior changes. Eventually the family recognizes that Phyllis has an alcohol problem. Viewers learn about alcohol problems in later life and how to intervene.

Publication Price : $ 50.00 each

Publication Price : $ 300.00 per set from Oregon State University. http://extension.oregonstate.edu/fcd/aging/extpubs.php

And I heard a loud voice saying, "Now the dwelling place of God is with men and he shall live with them. They will be his people, and God himself will be with them and be their God. He will wipe every tear from their eyes. There will be no more death or mourning or crying or pain, for the old order of things has passed away.

*Revelation 21:3-4*

CHAPTER *10*

# STRANGERS AND ALIENS

**KEY THOUGHT: As we age we may feel like strangers and aliens in this world. We begin to feel less connected to our own neighborhood and family life and desire something that is hard to define. We come to see this as a letting go in order to prepare for life in the eternal kingdom of God.**

As humans we desire a place of belonging. Many of us have belonged to a work place, neighborhood community or church family. We have had our loved ones around us and have established traditions that bind us to them. As we age we begin to feel displaced, almost like strangers and aliens to our own world. Others have taken over and we have moved (or been moved) aside. The things that used to bring us such pleasure now seem dull and over-rated. The world seems to be hurling in a direction that no longer makes sense to us. For some, the increase in technology has created new means of communication that mystify. It seems impossible to keep abreast of the latest developments. Our "place of belonging" no longer seems like home and our hearts long for somewhere that is hard to define. This longing may make us impatient with the status quo. My mother used to say over and over, "I don't know why the Lord just doesn't take me. I am more than ready to go. I don't serve any purpose here anymore." Those around us try to pull us back not wanting to let us go. But often we are "gone", long before we've gone. Anticipation and hope draw our thoughts to what heaven must be like. We long to see Jesus and those who have gone on before us. However, it is important to trust God for the fullness of his timing and use our presence here well until the last breath draws the curtain on this life and opens on the next.

# LESSON 10, DAY 1
## LOOKING FOR A COUNTRY

**GRACE:** *That I might understand that my desires will not be fully met in this world but in the next.*

**SCRIPTURE:** Hebrews 11: 13-16

## MEDITATION QUESTIONS:

1) Who are "all these people" who did not receive the promise?

2) Where is the country that these people are looking for? Why have they chosen it rather than return to the familiar?

3) What has God done for these aliens and strangers? What might this city be like?

## FOR YOUR CONSIDERATION:

As we come closer to the end of life, it is easy to think that the Lord has not given us those things that he has promised—good health, blessings beyond measure, love that never ends. A bitterness can enter in tainting all that we do. It may make us cynical or crabby. The saints in the hall of faith were those that recognized that not everything would be given us in this world. They knew about being strangers and aliens in this land. They exhibited their great faith in knowing that God had prepared an eternal place for them and that promises are still waiting to be fulfilled. True faith fills us with anticipation and hope. We understand that everything that has happened here in this world was to prepare us for the place God has prepared for us. Jesus said, "In my Father's house are many mansions. I go to prepare a place for you that where I am there ye may be also." As the time grows closer no wonder we are like young children awaiting Christmas. How long Lord? Will this be the day?

**FOR JOURNALING:** Do you have unfulfilled desires that you have abandoned because you know they will not be filled in this life? Discuss. Do you believe that fulfillment is awaiting you in "another country"?

_____

_____

_____

_____

_____

_____

_____

_____

_____

_____

_____

_____

_____

_____

_____

_____

_____

_____

_____

_____

_____

_____

_____

_____

# LESSON 10, DAY 2
## HIS LOVE ENDURES FOREVER.

**GRACE:** *To understand that all creation will be freed from bondage to decay into glorious freedom.*

**SCRIPTURE:** Romans 8:18-25

## MEDITATION QUESTIONS:

1) What would it be like to live in a world completely free from sin and destruction?

2) What do you think it will be like to have your body redeemed and to experience fulfillment as the adopted children of God?

3) Are you waiting patiently for what you do not yet have? Discuss.

## FOR YOUR CONSIDERATION:

We look around us and see God's creation in a mess. Beautiful animals are becoming extinct because their homelands have been demolished in the name of progress. Our lands are filled with plastic garbage. Our earth suffers from pesticides dangerous to all who injest them. Breathing disorders are on the increase, and cities are enveloped with pollution because we have insisted on fast, long distance transport. Our ocean is in danger from oil spills that coat the beautiful sea creatures with black. Indeed, our creation is groaning, longing for something better. It is wonderful to know that we are not alone in desiring a rebirth for creation. Our God the Creator also longs for this and has plans to make it happen. We can hardly imagine a world without sin, evil, and destruction. But imagine a place with no violence, where the lamb lies down with the lion, where skin color no longer separates us, and where our God walks and talks with us. Remember, our present sufferings are not to be compared with the glory that will be revealed.

**FOR JOURNALING:** Describe your own longing for renewal of our earth. Describe you longing for the redemption of your own body. Do you believe it will happen? Why or why not?

_____

_____

_____

_____

_____

_____

_____

_____

_____

_____

_____

_____

_____

_____

_____

_____

_____

_____

_____

_____

_____

_____

_____

_____

# LESSON 10, DAY 3
## WE DO NOT LOSE HEART.

**GRACE:** *To not lose heart as the outward is wasting away.*

**SCRIPTURE:** 2 Corinthians 4:1-18

## MEDITATION QUESTIONS:

1) What does it mean for Christians to let light shine out of darkness?

2) What is treasure residing in clay jars?

3) Why are our outward troubles to be considered light & momentary?

## FOR YOUR CONSIDERATION:

Many things reinforce the idea that once the body starts to deteriorate we might as well be dead. It is easy to be in despair thinking of all of our unfulfilled hopes and dreams. It is also easy to concentrate on the discomforts and pain we experience. The believer should not, however, follow this pattern. Paul tells us that under no circumstance are we to lose heart because this outer decay is only a light and momentary passageway into eternal glory. He also sees this not as something to be simply endured but an opportunity to let the light of Christ shine through us. "We are hard pressed on every side, but *not crushed*; perplexed, but *not in despair*; persecuted, but *not abandoned*; struck down but *not destroyed*." When others are despairing in old age, we are to be a light that witnesses to the always faithful love of God. We are to let it be known that we do not consider life to be ending but simply transitioning to another phase in a far country. "This world is not my homeland, In tents I pass my days; T'ward yonder shore of glory, With yearning eyes I gaze; While seeks the world its folly, I view the citadel, Where free from care and sorrow, Forever I shall dwell" [*In Heaven All Is Gladness*, Stanza 2]
160

**FOR JOURNALING:** How does looking forward to future glory help you to be steadfast in the present?

_____

_____

_____

_____

_____

_____

_____

_____

_____

_____

_____

_____

_____

_____

_____

_____

_____

_____

_____

_____

_____

_____

_____

_____

_____

_____

# LESSON 10, DAY 4
## A CHOSEN PEOPLE

**GRACE:** *To rejoice in our inheritance as the adopted children of God through Jesus Christ.*

**SCRIPTURE:** 1 Peter 1:3-9; 2:9-12

## MEDITATION QUESTIONS:

1) What are we to be looking toward as the adopted children of God?

2) What does our adoption into the people of God mean to our status in this life?

3) What does Peter say about suffering all kinds of trials?

## FOR YOUR CONSIDERATION:

Peter is writing to people in the midst of severe danger. Life from day to day is uncertain. There is a good chance they might die in a horrible manner. He encourages them by reminding them that this world is not their real home. They are strangers and aliens living in a hostile land. He reminds them that even if they were to die, they have an inheritance awaiting them in heaven that can never perish, spoil or fade. They may have to endure sufferings and trials for the time being, but once it is over, eternity awaits. Once they were of no account but now they are the people of God having received mercy through Jesus Christ. While we may not be eaten by lions, death is not always easy for us either. Peter reminds us as well that the "hell" we have on earth is all of hell we will ever know. It will pass and a heavenly inheritance awaits us. Christian martyrs have died glorious deaths expressing fully their belief and hope in another world prepared for them by Jesus himself. We too can greatly rejoice and live in hope as chosen people of God awaiting our indestructable inheritance.

**FOR JOURNALING:** Many people say that they do not fear death but fear dying. What do you think about this? How might this passage of scripture help you?

_____

_____

_____

_____

_____

_____

_____

_____

_____

_____

_____

_____

_____

_____

_____

_____

_____

_____

_____

_____

_____

_____

_____

_____

_____

_____

# LESSON 10, DAY 5
## JUST IMAGINE

**GRACE:** *To anticipate the wonders of the new heaven and earth where God dwells with his people.*

**SCRIPTURE:** Revelation 21:1-8

## MEDITATION QUESTIONS:

1) What are we told about the new heaven and the new earth?

2) Who will experience the joys of the new heaven and new earth?

3) Who will be barred from the new heaven and new earth?

## FOR YOUR CONSIDERATION:

It is difficult for us to imagine what life would be like with the total absence of evil and its consequences. The little we are told wets our appetites. Imagine a city more beautiful than the most glorious bride. Imagine God walking once again with us in the gardens of the new earth. Imagine a place with no pain. Imagine God wiping away all tears that remain from our earthly life experience. Imagine no death or mourning. Imagine being filled with clear, clean water at no cost, and food grown without weeds or thorns. These wonderful promises are not meant to make us escape the realities of life on this earth. They are to make us more able to endure those realities with steadfast faith and joyous praise. It is easier for us to endure hardship if we know that there will be an ending and things will get better. We are overcome when we have no hope, nothing to anticipate. God has graciously provided us with a hint of what is to come. Its description is limited because there are no words to adequately describe the wonders and blessings we will know. Let us face all our days with bold courage and radiant hope, for he who overcomes will be rewarded with an unimaginable inheritance!

**FOR JOURNALING:** What are the evils you will be glad *not* to see in heaven? Can you imagine a life without them?

# ALL THIS AND A FUTURE TOO?

*Psalm 90; 2 Samuel 7:18-29; Revelation 22:12-16*

Moses writes Psalm 90 after the Israelites have built and worshiped a golden calf. Moses had gone up on the mountain to talk with God and receive the laws of the covenant for the people, but they had tired of waiting and decided to construct their own way of doing "religion." They melted down all their valuables and under the direction of Aaron, the people built an image to worship instead of waiting for the real thing. Moses recognizes God's anger and pleads that God relent and set aside his boiling anger and frustration at this wayward people. He prays that they may once again know his compassion and unfailing love. He prays that the people will use their time wisely (number their days) and that God would establish the work of their hands instead of the people taking the work into their own hands to build imitation gods.

In David's prayer we see that God answered Moses' prayer. The enemies have been driven out and the kingdom has been established. God has promised David that his throne will last forever. This promise is fulfilled in the reign of Jesus the Christ. David asks "Who am I?" and "Who are these people that you have brought us this far and prepared a future for us as well?" It is an awesome thing to consider when you ponder the history of both the man and the people. Both histories are filled with missteps and rebellion. David was a sinful man and Israel was a sinful nation. Countless times the nation had fallen away from the true God to worship their neighbor's gods, suffered the consequences and pled with the Lord to forgive their wayward behavior and once again be their God. David himself fell away from God to commit adultery and murder. We have a wonderful record of his prayer for forgiveness and restoration in Psalm 51.

We can identify with David's prayer in 2 Samuel. Who am I? Who are we who call ourselves Christian? We are a sinful people who have fallen short of the glory of God. How amazing that he should show us his unfailing love and compassion. We too take the works of God into our own hands only to build "golden calves" in place of living in covenant with our God. Like David we can look back in amazement that God continues his relationship with us. "Through many trials and dangers we've already come, . . . we've no less days to sing God's praise than when we first begun"(Amazing Grace). We remember the ways in which he has

166

conquered our enemies and brought us out of danger into safety. We remember how through Jesus Christ he has forgiven our rebellions and reestablished our footing. We remember the blessings he has showered along the way and we are overcome. Indeed, who are we that he should do this for us? And not only this but he has prepared a future for us as well! David was told that there would be a wonderful house in which the Lord would dwell built by his family—a glorious temple. The temple that David built did not last forever but the temple of our God is a holy city more beautiful than words can describe. Jesus tells us that "In my Father's house are many mansions and I go to prepare a place for you." We look back at God's undeserved goodness to us and say with David "All this and a future too?" We are stunned at the goodness of our God. May we, like Moses, number our days and establish the works of our hands under the direction of our God as we await the glorious future he has prepared for us. ‡ [SCE]

## A SONG OF HEAVEN AND HOMELAND

—Eben E. Rexford

Sometimes I hear strange music,
Like none e'er heard before,
Come floating softly earthward
As thro' Heav'n's open door:
It seems like angel voices,
In strains of joy and love,
That swell the mighty chorus
Around the throne above.
**Refrain**
O sweet, celestial music,
Heard from a land afar—
The song of Heav'n and Home-
land,
Thro' doors God leaves ajar!

Now soft, and low, and restful,
It floods my soul with peace,
As if God's benediction
Bade all earth's troubles cease.
Then, grander than the voices
Of wind, and wave, and sea—
It fills the dome of Heaven
With glorious harmony.
**Refrain**

This music haunts me ever,
Like something heard in dreams—
It seems to catch the cadence
Of heav'nly winds and streams.
My heart is filled with rapture,
To think, some day to come,
I'll sing it with the angels—
The song of Heav'n and home.
**Refrain**

# GROUP QUESTIONS

*1) Describe the ways in which you feel alienated from the culture in which we live.*

*2) Do you long for this earth to be better? Do you long for another country? Discuss.*

*3) How might these feelings be a way that God prepares you for death?*

*4) How will the new heaven and earth differ from the one we live in now?*

*5) Who will be the inhabitants of the new heaven and new earth?*

*6) Describe what it means to be the people of God, inhabiting a different kingdom.*

*7) Read Hebrews 11 and 12. What does it tell us about the saints of God who have gone on before us?*

*8) What does the Hebrews passage tell us about the total fulfillment of God's promises to us?*

## ADDITIONAL ACTIVITIES

1) **GROUP:** Using your local paper, look at the articles and make a note of all the ways in which all life on earth is groaning and awaiting renewal.

2) **GROUP MEMBER:** Make a list of things that have changed in the last ten years. Journal your feelings in regard to these changes. Which of these make you hopeful and which make you fearful for the future of this earth.

3) **GROUP MEMBER:** Using pictures from magazines, make a collage that shows the life you anticipate in the new heaven and the new earth. In contrast make one that shows all the anti-kingdom things that will no longer exist. Bring your collages to share with your group members.

4) **GROUP MEMBERS:** Bring your favorite music (hymn, praise song, anthem, etc) that talks about after-life in God's kingdom. (i.e. This world in not my home, I'm just a passing through; Marching to Zion; Imagine etc.) Share a part of the song with the group.

# RESOURCES

[Please note: while I have read many of the books, visited web sites, and viewed videos that I have listed as resources, I have not read, used or viewed them all. Some of them have been chosen from reviews and excerpts on Amazon.com, brief overviews online, and recommendations from friends. These books have been selected to cross denomination lines. Check the publisher to select those that would best serve your group. I hope you find them useful in your study of the subject. ▯ This symbol indicates that the book is reviewed in the book review section.]

## BOOKS AND ARTICLES:

*The Glory of Heaven*, John F. MacArthur, Crossway Books.

*Heaven*, Randy Alcorn, Tyndale House, 2004.

*A Peculiar People*, Rodney Clapp, IVP Academic, 1966.

*Resident Aliens: Life in the Christian Colony*, Stanley Hauerwas and William H. Willimon, Abingdon Press, 1989

*We Shall See God: Charles Spurgeon's Classic Devotional Thoughts on Heaven*, Randy Alcorn, Tyndale, 2011.

## WEB VIDEOS, ARTICLES AND SITES OF INTEREST:

## MOVIES AND DVDS:

*Heaven, One Minute After You Die*, a Day of Discovery Program.

*What Dreams May Come*, starring Robin Williams [This is Hollywood's idea of afterlife. It would make an interesting discussion about the truth and fiction regarding the afterlife.]

# BOOK REVIEWS

# Summoned At Every Age
*Peter van Breemen*
*Notre Dame, Indiana, Ave Maria Press, 2005. #3 in the Ignatian Impulse Series*

Peter van Breemen is an experienced Jesuit leader of retreats, born in 1927, and now living in Germany. He has written several books on spiritual growth. In the preface of this book he writes "Aging is a gift. But if it is a gift it is also a task: a multifaceted and complex task." He offers this brief book in the hope that it "will help many people experience harmony and fruitfulness during the sometimes difficult final stage of their lives." Breeman writes as if he were a loving father, pointing to ways in which all of us experience the loving care of God, the Father.

The book is engaging and easy to read. He is refreshingly candid about the difficulties of the task, yet with a strong belief in the grace of God to take us through those days. He offers simple, yet profound advice on how we are to do our part. Illness in the final days may be painful, yet those who are suffering still possess dignity. Their experience points beyond themselves, and in so doing serves others. Even though we may suffer, we may accept God's gift of himself and be grateful. We can continue to pray, even though our prayer may become quieter and quieter. We are to surrender to God as Jesus said "Father into your hands I commend my spirit."

We are to give and receive forgiveness. Mutual forgiveness is perhaps the "most important contribution to the clarity we need in order to peacefully and confidently complete the final stretches of our lives." As we approach death, we are to be confident in the everlasting love of God for us. Yet people close to death may well feel lonely and so it is incumbent upon those who care for these people to demonstrate compassion.

This is a gentle book, full of wisdom, grounded firmly in the Jesuit tradition. [LFB]

## WINTER SOULSTICE, CELEBRATING THE SPIRITUALITY OF THE WISDOM YEARS
*John Killinger*
*New York: The Crossroad Publishing Company, 2005.*

In this spiritual autobiography, this wise, talented, teacher, prolific author (some fifty books) and preacher, shares with us his musings on high and low points of his long life. From his early days as a Southern Baptist a preacher at a tiny church in rural Kentucky to his retirement years, he remembers events, and people who have shaped his life, who have made him the person he is today.

While the book is mostly about the author, he says it is really about the idea "that in our elder years everything about us, our stored memories and experiences, our choices and our failure to choose, our friendships and associations, all come together like the tributaries of a river to form the spiritual beings into which we have evolved." He has thought about that construct most all his life. He has the insights to bring his off. His formal education certainly helped—doctorates in English Literature and then Theology in prestigious institutions, lots of educational travel, plenty of time for reflection, and a gift for writing as he went along. He talks a lot about his progression of faith. Finally, he asserts, "we learn to love ourselves for God's sake," but first we must sort out our lives and "know who it is we are loving."

In contrast to his serious, practical side which dominates, he rejoices in playfulness. He loved vacations and made many trips to Europe, England even to Vietnam while Seoul was being shelled. Joy, diversion, excitement have added to who he is in his senior years.

His work, or calling, was central; he loved it, even from his childhood years. He found joy in his work, except perhaps when he had a brief stint as an academic dean. His most joy was teaching in the divinity school at Vanderbilt. He says, "We are, in some ways, what we have done. It is a good feeling. It is an offering to God."

He admits to having a "Don Quixote" complex. He illustrates it by a story of a prolonged conflict he had with Jerry Falwell when he went to Lynchburg, Virginia, as minister at the First Presbyterian Church. Falwell was at the height of his empire and Killinger preached a sermon that roused the ire of that evangelical giant. The conflict went on for five years After Killinger had moved as a teacher to Samford University the conflict continued and when he was barred from the teaching he had wanted to do, he brought legal action against the school, but finally dropped it and resigned.

There is much more I'd love to share, but just this final recitation. Killinger tells of an encounter he had as a youth with the angel Gabriel. He was on his knees in prayer and he was aware of another presence in the small room. He saw this "spectral being" as tall as the room, with light appearing to come from inside him. Neither said a word and soon Gabriel was gone. When Killinger finally figured it out he was convinced that he had received an extraordinary gift, "an anchor for life." Several times in the years ahead he thrived on the recollections of that event. Then he saw Gabriel many years later in another vision.

He claims that the theme of the ministry in the churches he served "was seeking union with the holy." In summing up he concludes "I feel as if I am somehow melding with God and becoming an indistinguishable part of the totality of all that is…my heart is filled with indescribable joy." He thanks God for this gift and hopes that we can recognize this process happening in our own lives.

May all the glory be to God. [LFB]

## AGING AS A SPIRITUAL JOURNEY
*Eugene C. Bianchi*
*New York, New York, The Crossroad Publishing Company, 1997*

Bianchi is Professor Emeritus of Religion at Emory. He is now in his mid-seventies, having retired in 2000 after thirty two years of teaching. He has written several books on aging, and a significant sociological study of American Jesuits, relying on extensive interviews. He has also written a sizzling novel, *The Bishop of San Francisco, Romance, Intrigue and Religion.* He took the lead in establishing The Emeritus College at Emory.

In this book Bianchi attempts to establish a general framework for a spirituality of aging. It is a scholarly book, yet accessible to any thoughtful reader. He writes from a Christian perspective in a broad sense with excursions into Judaism and eastern religions. Bianchi admits to being influenced by Jungian psychology and blends cultural, psychological, social-science, and theological elements in the various chapters.

The book is more or less equally divided between challenges, potential, and reflections first for middle age and then for elderhood. He includes interviews with midlife and elder men and women, bringing an intensely personal flavor to the book.

In the chapters on midlife, Bianchi invites us to move toward a more contemplative existence, to develop an attitude of prayer as a way of "dwelling at the core of our being." He sees the potential for transformation of the self and of a new attitude toward work. He stresses the need for a group for caring and support. The summons in midlife is to "new levels of human-spiritual transcendence."

There is depth and creative insight in this book. These are just a few of his observations on elderhood. We are challenged to change our image of what it means to be old. We are encouraged to assess our gifts, and to face the reality of death. Growth, he argues, will come from what he calls "diminishment." Such growth requires faith and hope. And undergirds the self's creative potential in old age. Self assessment is necessary. We are to grow in creativity and wisdom.

We are encouraged to look inward and to "reidentify" ourselves, to meet previously unaddressed needs. Inner explorations, service to others, a greater integration of the whole person, are our tasks. We are encouraged to review our lives and to prepare for death. I was struck by his advice that we are to learn the "compassion and forgiveness of the wounded healer." We are to live in the present, not the past, and to participate in the transformation of the world. Some challenging, powerful advice.

In the final chapter of interviews people share their thoughts on confronting death and on life after death. Some sobering, thought provoking insights. If you want to go deep into the subject of the spirituality of aging, this book is for you. [LFB]

## LIVING SIMPLY IN AN ANXIOUS WORLD
*Robert J. Wicks*
*Mahwah, N.J., Paulist Press, 1988*

The world is in turmoil; it is indeed an anxious time. Wicks, with a doctorate in psychology, specializes in the treatment and mentoring of professional helpers. In this short book, he shares insights and practical ways to live simply and meaningfully.

He challenges, and encourages. He reminds us that we often lose our way; we forget that God has one expectation for us: to love. Wicks makes one essential assumption about those who say they commit to love. They must believe with certainty that Jesus was indeed God incarnate, that he was resurrected and that he is "there" for us.

But how can we love? Well, we must act. We are blocked by our attitudes, approach to life, by negative patterns of life. These are hard to break. For example, we may be depressed and unable to love. We must take the initiative to break these patterns.

We must, Wicks argues, address cognition (styles of thinking, perceiving, and understanding), imagery, behavior, and affect (feeling, mood or emotions). Wick combines the psychological and the spiritual as he examines these four issues.

We must listen to God's voice, in so doing we get beyond protecting or crucifying ourselves and hear the voice of love. Grounded in hope based on the resurrection of Christ we see all things new, including ourselves. Then our behavior, our service to God, is transformed. We see the love hidden in our hearts, all interactions are opportunities, made manifest through constant prayer. Prayer allows us to experience God in a personal, transforming way.

The chapters are entitled Listening (Cognition), Seeing(Imagery), Service(Behavior), and Experiencing (Affect). He shares many thoughtful ideas and practical ideas. I'll share just a bit from the chapter on Service. "Compassion is a hidden attitude of love. Our actions make visible this love." Our actions open up our hearts to the truth. Openness is the key, "have low expectations and high hopes." Be open in each experience to the presence of God, to holiness. There is symbolic greatness in small, caring actions, even presences. Share a smile, a few words of caring. A gentle pat on the back. Be active, but not busy. Don't let yourself be overwhelmed, so that you put people off. We are to be in touch with our own humanness, care for ourselves, love; do something because it is the natural thing to do, not out of a sense of guilt. We may feel doubt, failure, hostility, even a void. Then we must pray.

In his last chapter, "Deadly Clarity" Wicks really "socks it to us." He writes "From a psychological perspective, sin is primarily the result of denying, ignoring or worshiping our personality instead of nurturing it in light of the Gospel call to respond in faith, hope and love." God is in us; when we deny that, and let our feelings of depression, anxiety, insecurity and the like take charge we ignore the possibilities God holds out to us. In other words we let sin control us. True security comes from letting God be in charge. Let grace prevail. Encouraging words, tough ones, too. Letting go of the false promises is never easy.

Take a look at Wicks' book and be ready for a challenge. [LFB]

## When God Interrupts, Finding New Life Through Unwanted Change
*M. Craig Barnes*
*Downers Grove, Illinois, InterVarsity Press, 1996.*

Barnes is Pastor of the Shadyside Presbyterian Church in Pittsburgh, and Professor of Leadership and Ministry at the Pittsburgh Theological Seminary. Before coming to Pittsburgh in 2002 he was for nine years pastor at the National Presbyterian Church in Washington, DC. He has written several books in the area of spirituality and is a frequent conference leader.

He begins this book by reminding us that "we just keep losing things, wives, husbands, friends, health, the dreams and security of the past. Nothing stays the way it was." Most all of us have suffered some sort of loss that has left us feeling adrift. Some of us simply endure. Some find a new life. Jesus said things like "Only those who lose their lives will find them." Barnes points out that we who are Christians call this process "conversion." Drawing on his experience as a pastor, Barnes shares what is essentially a message of hope and joy.

My own life has not brought me any truly shattering losses. My wife and I have been together for over fifty years, our children are grown and well. My health is decent, we have income enough to meet our modest needs. What I have lost is my ability to hear anywhere near as well as I have in the past and some of my memory has left me. I do not have the full time engagement as a college administrator and have not found a truly fulfilling alternative. I am somewhat "at a loss." Barnes' thoughts about "unwanted change" struck a modest responsive chord with me.

While I sense I am on a downward journey in some relatively minor ways, Jesus suffered, in death on a cross: "My God, why have you forsaken me?" he cried. Paul suffered great losses, yet proclaimed that he counted "everything a loss compared to the surpassing greatness of knowing Christ Jesus my Lord." Barnes' challenge to me is to accept that my troubles are minor ones, and to move on, trusting in God to lead and to protect.

Barnes writes of several kinds of abandonment. Some people are abandoned by success. Careers go really sour, one is cast out on one's own and even major efforts yield no results. One man, having retired early, uncertain what to do, decided to launch a new venture in community development with a Black church in his town. He came to believe that Jesus had led him to a place he had not wanted to go, but that it became a better place.

Some people are abandoned by good health. While some degree of brokenness is an essential characteristic of being human, it is also our best opportunity to live with the Saviour. Barnes himself was stricken with a serious form of cancer just as he was to take on a major new call. He figured that all would be well, but it was not, the spreading disease persisted. He believed he was too important to God for cancer to take him so early. But then his perspective changed, he accepted the reality that he needed God; God did not need him. Grace came to him. He recalled the wrestling match between Jacob and God. Jacob finally saw God; it was what he needed, he made peace with life.

There are those who are abandoned by family and even by God or so they may think. But, it is the false image of God that we have let go and when we accept that then we are free to discover more of the mystery of God. Maybe we look to God to respond to challenges we face, and when we do not get the response we seek maybe we even begin to question if we really believe even as we go through all the right motions, attending worship, helping to feed the hungry. Maybe we think we know a lot about God, and yet do not really know Him.

Barnes helps us work through such circumstances. For him the essential message came from a frail, elderly woman in a nursing home when he went there to serve her communion. She prayed with him, saying

"Thank you God for being so good to me. Thank you that I am not forgotten. Thank you for always loving me." We are to live lives of gratitude. We are invited to go on a passionate journey with God. Be grateful. Barnes can help us know how to do that. [LFB]


## THE WAY OF TRANSITION, EMBRACING LIFE'S MOST DIFFICULT MOMENTS
*William Bridges*
*Cambridge, MA: Perseus Books Group, 2001.*

I admit it up front: I am of two minds about this book. I've been interested in career development for many years and in the changes people have made in their ways of "making a living." I was aware that most folks find it difficult to change. So, reading something about transitions seemed attractive to me. On the other hand, the author's approach was so blatantly self-centered I got impatient. But I determined to calm down and share some of the insights of this thoughtful analysis of the way of moving from one phase of life to another.

First, some background of the author. He taught English at the higher education level, and in the mid-1970s shifted to the field of transition management (a new field). He wrote several books on the subject, gave lectures and workshops, and made a name for himself in helping people move through transitions in their lives. He was married for nearly forty years to a practicing psychotherapist who died of cancer. For many years he and his wife followed parallel, related careers. For part of his life he consulted with a psychotherapist, as well. And he and his wife loved to talk with each other. He continued his service as a consultant and writer on the theme of transitions throughout his life.

Earlier books had explored the issue of transitions in great depth, and he had written on job change, as well. In this book he expands his insights, but also, and this is new, shares his own personal history of professional and personal transitions with remarkable candor. I sometimes felt I was listening to his personal revelations I really should not be hearing. His point in this expose was to link his theory and his own experience in a way that was not only helpful to him, but he estimated, would be to others as well.

Transition, he explains, is not change. Change triggers transition. We experience reorientation, personal growth, authentication and creativity. Authentication may be hardest of these to grasp. It is, the author says, "the inner face of growth, where the result is not just appropriate but is also a way of being that is true to who we really are, rather than to a persona or role." Moving through a transition means first of all, letting go of those aspects of our life which hold us back. For a time we are in what Bridges calls the "neutral zone", where the present and the future are not clear. It may take some time and help to move through this zone. Bridges shares some personal exercises for the reader to help clarify what is going on within us. We need to accept the time of ending, let the neutral zone take over and to be ready to seize the opportunity to make a new beginning when that moment presents itself.

Bridge's marriage to Mondi, to hear his "side" of the relationship, was rich and rewarding and yet also deeply disappointing and difficult. There were deep personality differences which they lived with for many years. These times were ones of transition for Bridges. Once Mondi was afflicted with cancer much of his time was caring for her. Her death was a clear break in the past for Bridges, but after about a year and a half he fell in love with a woman eighteen years younger. They married and a new frontier opened for Bridges. In fact, this book is dedicated "To Susan…and a new beginning."

Bridges does a commendable job of weaving together his personal story and his considerable theoretical insights. And, as well, he provides some helpful suggestions for the reader to do some analysis of one's own experience with transition.

In conclusion, I confess that part of my emotional reaction to the book was the realization that I have not done as well as I would like in working through my own transitions. Doing so is a challenge. I have tried: I wrote a memoir in which I described my move from college teacher to academic administrator and activist for curricular change, to a retiree. But I admit I did not come to terms with the personal dynamic of the transitions with the insight yearned for. Maybe I'll try again. Then again, maybe not.

Read this book and see if you are up to it. [LFB]

# The Seasons of a Restless Heart
*Debra K. Farrington*
*San Francisco, Jossey-Bass, 2005*

I loved this book. No preaching, just simple, personal; from one restless heart to another. The frontpiece quotes Psalm 31:21 "Blessed be the Lord! For he has shown me the wonders of his love in a besieged city." Ms. Farrington, a popular retreat leader, church woman and sensitive interpreter of the Bible, was diagnosed with multiple sclerosis in the midst of writing this book. She persevered, a blessing for all of us.

The author begins with the stories of the Exodus and links those with our contemporary experiences of transition. Transition is the major theme of this gift of love. We all live through transitions, many of them, and Debra helps us to make sense of them, to accept them, to grow, mature.

"For everything there is a season" we are reminded by the writer of Ecclesiastes. Transitions are a part of our lives. Loss of a job, death of a spouse, children move away, we move far from home, a chronic illness. Many of the transitions we experience, the author tells us "dump us—sometimes rather unceremoniously—flat into an unsettled time, a restless season." Farrington guides us through the endings, the beginnings and most important, the long stretch of time between.

A friend here at the retirement center to which my wife and I moved a bit over two years ago, asked whether I had adjusted to retirement. I answered "yes" far too quickly. While I have been retired from a major administrative position in higher education for over a dozen years, I had to admit at the "feeling" level, that I still felt restless. I kept busy for three years soon after retirement as president of the local Habitat for Humanity affiliate, breaking in our first executive director. It was then time to start talking to my transition. I did not do a very good job in that conversation. I see now that I did not even consider following my heart as Farrington advises us to do. She gives suggestions, including spiritual practices and prayers. Praying and journaling are central to the exploration.

Transitions are uncomfortable, but they are also opportunities for creativity, to something new. God plants the seeds, it is up to us to water them, to see that they grow. We also look for signs. There was a great example of an opportunity coming to me in the midst of a major transition. I had left a major administrative position where I had served for 23 years. I was in something of a muddle, a time of restlessness, uncertainty. Our telephone rang and a man who identified himself as the president of a university in Florida urged me to come to DeLand to consider the position of Provost at Stetson University. I went, my wife went, and we came. This became a time of great opportunity as President Lee was determined to make some major advances, one I knew I could handle. After six years hiring many bright, creative faculty and helping to create a culture welcoming to women and minorities I decided to move on.

A big transition for me; no longer a major administrative position. Farrington writes about needing help; giving thoughtful ideas about how to move through restless times. She advises us to eat, sleep and exercise properly. After the author was diagnosised with multiple sclerosis, she had a major challenge. She writes of how she dealt with this reality. It helped her a lot simply to be silent, to listen, if only for five minutes a day, practice listening for God's word. Be silent, listen for God's word. She has several suggestions about questions to explore, thoughts about moving forward. Helpful exercises to settle and direct our thinking.

The last chapter of the book bears the title "Home Again." After so many years in the desert the Israelites stood at the edge of Canaan, ready to enter the promised home. There is relief, anticipation, but also the realization that there are new challenges, new delights. As we enter into the later years of our lives, we are apt to find ourselves in new homes. Maybe in new communities; maybe in a retirement community, or living with family. Life is beginning again.

For me, becoming a member of a retirement community certainly was a new beginning. On reflection I realize I did not fully accept that reality. It was time for me to reaffirm my faith, and to act on that faith. The transition to a new life is still going on for me. What I need to do is to be patient, to be gentle with myself, to accept the limitations aging has brought, and to listen to God speaking and to accept all the help I can get from those who care for me. I am encouraged by Farrington's final words "May you find yourself in a new place, flowing freely someday, at home again in the world and renewed." So may it be for all of us. [LFB]

# SIMPLICITY. THE FREEDOM OF LETTING GO
*Richard Rohr*
*New York, The Crossroads Publishing Company, 2003*

Richard Rohr is a Franciscan priest, born in Kansas in 1943. He was the founder of the New Jerusalem Church in Cincinnati in 1971 and in 1986 founded the Center for Action and Contemplation in Albuquerque, New Mexico. He serves as the Director of the Center and writes and lectures widely on spirituality.

This book grew out of lectures and essays and focuses on how we gain freedom as we let go of long-held beliefs and practices. He shares some radical ideas, provokes our thought, and points us to action and contemplation. Rohr challenges us in ways that are sure to make us very uncomfortable if we take him seriously. He is hard not to take seriously, yet few of us are likely to follow his injunctions.

In this commentary on "Simplicity" I will focus on what he urges us to do, especially what to give up. We are not so much in need of love as we are of wisdom. We need to take a radical journey inward and outward. We need to be free from ourselves, to renounce the need to be right, to give up a cerebral comprehension of God and to move to "emptiness." The way to move to forgiveness is to self-surrender, let go of our own slavery, let go of our possessions, give up our dependence on the "system." We have become so addicted to the "system," the economic and political system, that we don't even realize we have surrendered to it and in the process have given up our devotion to the Lord.

If the church is to be reformed it will be from below, from the poor, the dispossessed, the infirm, those who Jesus showed special concern for while he was on this earth. Rohr points to four forms of poverty in the Bible. 1) There is the poverty of sin, (the person is empty and missing the truth); 2) There is the poverty of oppressed men and women, 3) The poverty of the simple and humble life; (we are to put our trust not in possessions, but in God and other people). 4) The fourth poverty is the realization of our own limitedness and weakness. Yet in the midst of these poverties, Jesus tells us we are blessed.

Where does this lead us? Rohr argues that we need to be with and know those who are different from us, to see reality as they see it and then act. We are encouraged to give up thinking we are right. Listen to God speaking, let him tell us, go deep and find the truth. Open ourselves to God as an "earthquake", leading us to new ways of being.

Some of Rohr's most provocative thoughts focus on the impact of feminism. He writes:

"The language of patriarchy is always a noble or macho language of patriotism and freedom. ….The amazing thing is that anyone is still willing to believe it. But fortunately the poor, the oppressed and marginalized, and especially women, are beginning to trust their natural and truly religious instincts." And "The feminist insight is a rediscovery of Jesus' spirit, a reemergence of a well suppressed truth, an eventual political upheaval, a certain reform of our hearing of the Gospel and someday perhaps the very structures of the churches…" And one more quote "The feminist insight explains the vast majority of Jesus' teachings, a male acting very differently in an almost totally patriarchal Jewish society" Heavy stuff indeed and from a Franciscan.

Rohr wants us to live as sisters and brothers, in circles where we can be vulnerable and honest, and where healing and sharing are the hallmarks. He wants us to bring the truth of community and of individual freedom together. He sees a Christian as one who is "animated by the spirit of Christ, in whom the spirit of Christ can work."

His final chapter is entitled "Less is more." We are to "let go of the present…our self-image, our titles, our public image." We are to "recognize Christ in the least of our brothers and sisters." The issue is one of seeing. We are to find "authentic contemplation." When we find the "spacious place of the soul" we will "finally be at home." God is there too, and when we are there "we will have discovered simplicity."

Thus ends a most provocative commentary. Rohr seems to me to be speaking the Truth. Yet it is a truth that feels outside my grasp. Are you prepared to grasp the truth he advocates? [LFB]


# Necessary Losses, The Loves, Illusions, Dependencies, and Impossible Expectations That All of Us Have to Give Up in Order to Grow
*Judith Viorst*
*New York: The Free Press, 1986.*


And now for something completely different," as the host of a famous public television show of many years ago, used to say. This is a secular book, nary a mention of a life after this earthly life. Where is God, the reader may ask. Viorst, a poet, writer of children's books, and an earlier exploration of marriage, spent several years at the Washington Psychoanalytic Institute. This book is a product of her study and conversations over several years with many notable psychoanalysts. She claims not to be a strict Freudian, but also that she shares his belief that our past and the power of our unconscious shapes the events of our life. She is also convinced that recognizing what we are doing, and why, can expand our choices and possibilities.

She states her intention clearly: "central to understanding our lives is understanding how we deal with loss…..the people we are and the lives that we lead are determined, for better or worse, by our loss experiences." Coming to this understanding "can be the beginning of wisdom and hopeful change."

Viorst examines four major losses as we move through life.

—the losses in "moving away from the body and being of our mother and becoming a separate self";

—the losses "involved in facing the limitations on our power and potential and deferring to what is forbidden and what is impossible";

—"the losses of relinquishing our dreams of ideal relationships for the human relations of imperfect connections";

—"the multiple losses of the second half of life, of our final losing, leaving, letting go."

I found Viorst's observations cogent, challenging, believable, provocative, sometimes troublesome and when applied to my own experience, simply wrong. But I admit, I have not undergone psychoanalysis and so I have likely missed something. Obviously she is speaking in generalities about child-mother separation, as well as most of the losses associated with growing up. Her comments about sibling rivalry, about a slightly older child wondering when is mother going to take the new baby back, for example. And the struggles with adolescence, what losses we experience with those. These commentaries are fun to read and ponder. Where did they apply to my life, where do I see them happening with others now?

Viorst's chapter entitled "Love and Hate in the Married State" will strike home for many of us. The tensions and conflicts of married life surely begin with the romantic expectations many young couples bring to the marriage. The romantic and sexual disappointments many experience are losses that many couples find hard to overcome. As the author advises we can build our adult love, and preserve the imperfect connection known as marriage. In discussing children in marriage, Viorst confronts the unpleasant reality that some children are not loved all that much, that some get into big trouble, that some are abused. They will grow up and many will thrive, don't grieve over the losses we cannot control.

Viorist deals with the loss of loved ones. Some die young, some suddenly, some after long bouts with pain. People deal with death in various ways., some with denial, some with intense psychic pain, others with anger, guilt, some with idealization. The losses of death of a loved one are necessary and yet there may be long term harmful effects on the mental and physical health of the survivors. We have a choice, to live crippled or through the pain to forge "new adaptations." Accept the difficult changes and then "begin to come to the end of mourning."

Then we grow old. There are plenty of laments, the ears give out, the eyes as well; strength fades, the heart knows no peace, speech gives out and the mind fades. Some face these losses more vividly than others, but few escape completely. I volunteer in a nursing home each week and see many folks who have much cause to lament; some are cheerful. There are many losses as we grow old, but Viorst reminds us that we can transcend our own egos. We can feel pleasure in the pleasures of others, be concerned about events not directly related to our own self-interest and invest ourselves in tomorrow's world. We can find a new sense of aliveness.

Finally we come close to death. Viorst critiques Kubler- Ross's five stages of dying and offers her own observations. Some seek to end their own lives, some see death as a release, as a friend; some go quickly with no time for reflection. Some feel that our finite self is a part of something that endures, some believe in immorality. Maybe there is a literal afterlife or at least an immortal soul. This acknowledgement is the closest Viorst comes to the sort of life after death most Christians claim. [LFB]

# LEADERS GUIDE

# LEADER'S GUIDE
## INTRODUCTION

I hope you have had a chance to look over the course work, and have been challenged and excited by its possibilities. At first glance it may seem overwhelming to you. But let me reassure you that you are not expected to do everything suggested in a ten week period! You are the leader of the group and since you know the people you will be working with, you may feel free to pick and choose the material that best suits your people.

The unique format allows participants to spend a small block of time daily in the Word. They can mull over the questions concerning the biblical texts and then journal a personal question. By spending this reasonable amount of time daily they will bring thoughtfulness and insight to your group meeting.

Unlike many other small groups, this group is not about obtaining information or correct knowledge. The purpose of these small groups is to explore, create dialogue and share life experiences. It is important to create an atmosphere that is conducive to this. I like to set up a room that is like an after-dinner conversation. I use table clothes, candlelight, flowers, and provide refreshments. I give people time to chat with each other before the group begins its formal class. For many of your members, the social aspect is vital. They need to be with friends and it may be their only time out together.

I have suggested a number of movies and have found that it works to schedule a viewing at the church or one of the member's homes, serve popcorn and soft drinks, and make it a movie afternoon out. (Seniors often do not like to drive at night.) It is strongly recommended that the leader view the movie first and that he give the members a heads-up on the content. After the movie it is fun to have some questions ready to stimulate some conversation relating to the topic under discussion in the group.

As mentioned previously, there is a lot of material provided. The more your group members are willing to invest in the experience the more they will get out of it. You may have members who will fill in every question and read anything that is suggested, but unfortunately these are rare. At the other end, you may have members who never open their books between session but who like to speak "off the cuff"! It is important that *all* people feel welcomed regardless of how much they participate in the preparation for class. Please do not make any group member feel guilty for not having completed class preparation materials. Your group may stimulate a lot of thinking and processing that has nothing to do with writing anything down. Give the opportunity and let God do his work in each of the individuals in his own way.

## GROUP FORMATS

There are a number of ways that you may set up a group. First you need to decide if there is a specific length of time you wish to meet. There is enough material for a year's worth of small group meetings, if your group wants to stretch it out that long. Ask them what they see as a time investment.

One possibility is to meet weekly for 20 weeks. One class would introduce the Bible study and use the study questions. Members would go home and do the journaling and life integration work, coming back the following week to share in the group questions and activities.

Another possibility is to meet once a month for ten months. Begin and end with a social time. In the first half of the morning, do the Bible study, send people off to quiet corners to do the personal work, take a coffee break, and then gather to share through the group questions. If you did not have breakfast together you might consider having the members bring something to share for a pot luck lunch.

While it is possible to take each class time and cover what you can and pick up at the next class, I think on the whole it is best to keep the class moving and have a definite ending time.

The group size should be kept to no more than a dozen. Not everyone will attend every time, so your group will average ten or so and this will allow everyone a time to share. I have found in larger groups there is a reticence to share.

## SMALL GROUP GUIDELINES

In preparation for leading a group, I strongly suggest that you read: *A Hidden Wholeness* by Parker J. Palmer, John Wiley and Sons, Inc., 2004.

(This whole book is a wonderful discussion on creating a safe environment for small groups—groups where each person can be heard with respect and compassion. Groups where no one is wounded. Groups that grow in love rather than dissension.)

## TO BE A GOOD LISTENER

1) There is no need to fill every second of the time with talk. Allow some time for quiet consideration of what others have shared.

2) Be careful not to express a value judgment on what the speaker has shared. Even an "That was awesome," indicates that you approve or have been wowed by the persons comments thus indicating that what others have shared may not be so "awesome." A simple "thank you for sharing" lets the person know that you value the contribution no matter what you may have thought of the content.

3) It is difficult to share with a group when you are the only one who is being open and intimate in your sharing. The best way to show appreciation for someone's candid sharing, is by being equally open in your own sharing. A mutual sharing benefits all. If only one person is open in the sharing, that person may feel foolish for having been so candid and may decide not to share upon another occasion, thus robbing the group of valuable insight.

## ADDITIONAL SUGGESTIONS

1) These groups are not about fixing one another! Unless the speaker asks for suggestions none should be set forth. When one does respond it

is important that he/she share only their own experience. He/she should never tell another what they should or shouldn't do.

2) It is important that the leader not allow group sharing to decline into conflict or debate on controversial political, social, or religious issues. For example if a woman were to share about an abortion, it should not become an argument over pro-choice or anti-abortion views. The group should respect her with time and space to deal with her own thoughts and feelings on her own particular situation.

4) In dealing with personal issues there is no one overriding truth that can be used to govern all situations. We do not thrust forward "THE TRUTH" as if coming from on high. We trust the Holy Spirit to do its works in the hearts and minds of all who attend. Openness and attentiveness may help us all to grow in grace and the compassion of our Lord.

Another source of wisdom for small group is in the materials presented by 12 Step groups on cross talk. *It cannot be stressed strongly enough that lack of confidentiality will kill a group!*

A person must feel safe if they are to share the intimate details of their lives. What a person hears in group cannot become fodder for the church gossip mill. Nothing will hurt individuals or your church more. *As a leader you must yourself keep all information to yourself. Do not use the excuse of "praying for" to announce to non-group members (EVEN YOUR PASTOR) what you have been told in confidence without the member's permission. It is appropriate to say to a member "With your permission I would like to talk with the pastor about this." Or it is proper to suggest that the group member approach the pastor if there is a need for confession, reconciliation etc. You may also help the member to find resources such as counseling if you are approached for help. PERSONAL PRAYER FOR YOUR GROUP MEMBERS IS ALWAYS PROPER!* God works in strange and mysterious ways.

## FINAL COMMENTS

The resources I have listed are ones that I have come across. They are by no means exhaustive. I would appreciate any other suggestions that you come across, and encourage you to e-mail me with any comments or questions you have. I would love to have stories of your group to put on the web page. Also if your members have written short stories or poems that might be appropriate for the web page I would certainly consider posting them. This material is not cut in stone, so if you have found something to add or delete once again, please contact me at sescontrias@cfl.rr.com.

Each group will have a life of its own. It is important for the leader to be flexible yet rein the group in when necessary. Remember this is *to be a positive, life-giving experience*. Your goal for this unit is to help group members bring closure to their lives, to complete the tasks of forgiving and reconciliation, to bring blessing and final words to their friends and family, to develop a daily awareness, and to nurture a spirit of gratitude. Obviously this is not all going to be accomplished in the short period of time that your group meets, but your members can develop an awareness of what needs to be done and make a good start. Blessings on you!

# <u>ACKNOWLEDGMENTS</u>

It is with great gratitude that I acknowledge those who played a special part in this writing. First of all this project began with God's leading me to live with and accompany my elderly mother for six years as she progressed from moderate activity and mental acuity to frailty, senility and finally death. Her experience taught me how unprepared most of us are to deal with advancing age and dying. It was a first-hand window into aging's benefits, challenges and realities. Mother faced it bravely with the tools she had available. Thank you Mother.

There were individuals whose special encouragement as I began to pursue the idea of Autumn Saints meant so very much—Rev. Bruce Hedgepeth, Rev. Matt McCollum and Rev. Radford Rader; my sister Penelope Taylor who shares the journey with me and my special friend Renee Roeschley whose belief in the project and in me never wavered; Rev. Mike Murphy and Martha-Virginia Spivey who have continued to press me to finish this work; Jan Gray who graciously helped with the proofing; the first attendees of Autumn Saints groups who heartily engaged the material and gave their honest feedback; Covenant Publications—especially Rev. Jim Hawkinson, Jane Swanson-Nystrom, Steve Luce and David Westerfield for teaching me all I know about editing and desktop design; and the many who have used and responded to Autumn Saints materials. One gets into trouble at times like this—there is always the chance that with an aging memory someone's name will be omitted but nevertheless their influence is a part of the whole work of God. We are indeed God's workmanship and nothing is possible without Him.

Thanks are especially due to Lou Brakeman for his insightful book reviews. He has a unique gift for being able to connect the written words of others to our daily lives. He has been most gracious in sharing his wisdom and experience with us. He has been a wonderful mentor and role model for me. Thank you Lou!

Blessings to you who work this workbook. May God be in the process and use it to encourage, teach, and prepare you to make this period of your life the best yet. [SCE]

# NOTES

# NOTES

# NOTES

40183773R00116

Made in the USA
Lexington, KY
27 March 2015